ENGAGING IN TRANSCENDENCE

THE CHURCH'S MINISTRY AND COVENANT WITH YOUNG CHILDREN

Barbara Kimes Myers
William R. Myers

The Pilgrim Press
Cleveland, Ohio

The Pilgrim Press, Cleveland, Ohio 44115

© 1992 by The Pilgrim Press

Chapter 1 material from the book *The Keeping Quilt* by Patricia Polacco, © 1988 by Patricia Polacco, used by permission of the publisher, Simon & Schuster Books for Young Readers, New York, New York 10020. Parts of chapter 3 initially appeared as "Transcendence in the Pre-School: Supporting the Relationship Between the Pre-School and the Church" in *British Journal of Religious Education*, Summer 1987, 148–51. Parts of chapter 6 written as "Adults Intend for Worship to Be Hospitable for Children" by Donald Griggs and Patricia Griggs, © 1991. Used by permission.

Printed in the United States of America

The paper used in this publication is acid free and meets the minimum requirements of American National Standard for Information Sciences-Permanence of Paper for Printed Library Materials, ANSI Z39.48–1984

97 96 95 94 93 92   5 4 3 2 1

Cover design by Cindy Dolan.

Library of Congress Cataloging-in-Publication Data

Myers, Barbara Kimes, 1941–
    Engaging in transcendence : the church's ministry and convenant with young children / Barbara Kimes Myers, William R. Myers.
        p.   cm.
    Includes bibliographical references.
    ISBN 0-8298-0932-5 (alk. paper)
    1. Church work with children.   I. Myers, William, 1942– . II. Title.
BV639.C4M84   1992
259'.22—dc20   92-22223
                                                                      CIP

Linda Dalrymple Goddal

ENGAGING IN
TRANSCENDENCE

For Our Parents,
Alma and Norman L. Kimes,
Margaret and William A. Myers,
and their grandchildren,
and their grandchildren's children . . .

CONTENTS

FOREWORD

As one who has spent twenty-five of my more than thirty years of ministry in the local church, I cannot celebrate more enthusiastically the publication of this volume. Every pastor and local church ought to have this penetrating book on their shelves. It should not be there to collect dust but to be read and used as a resource for all who care about young children and our ministry to and with them. It should also be on seminary library shelves as a resource for ministerial studies. We owe a debt of gratitude to Barbara Kimes Myers and William R. Myers for their painstaking research, their practical involvement in programs for young children and youth, and their theological challenge to churches and other religious institutions.

There are times when one wonders whether many persons in the United States possess a commitment to children. Many persons speak of children, their needs, and their future, but when it comes to making those strategic decisions that place children as a number one priority in the distribution of our resources, they are often not high on the list. This is often true of public policy and, I must painfully admit, even of some church policy.

There should be no question for the church on how children should be regarded. Clearly Jesus challenges his followers: "Let the little children come to me, and do not stop them; for it is to such as these that the kingdom of heaven belongs" (Matt. 19:14). What a mandate for all who work with children. All children, including many who suffer a variety of abuses and woeful neglect, deserve a caring and nurturing atmosphere in which to grow, to dream, and to learn. Is this not what the church, temple, and other religious institutions claim to be about? Our passion for the lives of young children ought to spread from our faith communities to every child-caring institution and to society at large. Young children are among the most vulnerable persons in our nation and in the world. They need advocates and care givers, and, I might add, in many cases, so do their parents.

Too often in both government and church, when budgets have to be balanced, children suffer. Too many adults are willing to claim that they have finished the job of rearing children or are quick to say, "Those children are not my responsibility." The truth is that all children belong to the family of God, and we should care for and about them because we are a part of their extended families.

Churches and temples operate Sunday church schools, weekday religious schools, and early-childhood programs. The quality of such programs should be foremost in our minds as we go about nurturing the future's ethical and caring adults. I've often thought that if national or church religious bodies would declare a moratorium on all other programs for two years and focus on young children in every affiliated local church and temple, religion could have a major impact on national policy. This is not just a far-fetched idea. Think of the impact of such a stance on the development of child-care professionals, youth workers, parents, and families. Think of what it could mean for communities, cities, states, and this nation.

The Children's Defense Fund, led by that foremost advo-
cate for children, Marian Wright Edelman, has a prayer that
is widely used on all its materials. This prayer ought to be
one we repeat daily.

> *Dear Lord*
> *Be good to me.*
> *The sea is so wide and*
> *My boat is so small.*

Barbara and William Myers have provided a powerful
resource for persons who care for children. As we go about
the task of being God's agents in behalf of young children,
we need the thoughtful insights provided by this book.

KENNETH B. SMITH
Chicago Theological Seminary

PREFACE AND ACKNOWLEDGMENTS

This is a book about children, the church, and the church's ministry with young children. In writing this book, we have assumed *ministry* to be a lived response to God on the part of *every* Christian. This assumption has led us to claim that ministry is a central part of the Christian vocation and that those who care for, teach, nurture, heal, and invite young children into caring, covenantal relationships are engaged in a critically important ministry. "We" are two educators–church members who have been involved for many years within a variety of settings connected to the church's ministry with children. Barbara currently teaches graduates and undergraduates in the School of Education at DePaul University in Chicago. Bill teaches at Chicago Theological Seminary, where he is the academic dean. We are also the parents of three children: a college graduate, one who is in the middle of her college experience, and a college freshman.

Co-teaching a course at Chicago Theological Seminary with the same title as this book led to an invitation to deliver jointly a series of keynote addresses at one of San Francisco Theological Seminary's summer gatherings of preschool professionals and religious educators. Often such preschool professionals and religious educators use differing "languages" when they talk about what they do when they work with children. The former will name what occurs within the children's world, using concepts associated with education and child-development theory; the latter will be more comfortable using words from a biblical or theological frame of reference. But when a congregation contains a children's center or preschool run by preschool professionals who do not have an understanding of the church's ministry and a church school run by religious educators who lack an understanding of appropriate early-childhood education, often the end result is a prolonged "turf war" in which children are the real losers. In addition, while people who teach in the public sector and who provide care through social agencies and hospitals often consider themselves to be "in ministry," the church rarely affirms their vocation as being one of importance. So we prepared our keynote addresses for San Francisco with care, assuming that we had been charged with the further building of a conversation that was aware and respectful of the strengths and perspectives carried by both "sides." We also realized that ministry with young children can be conceived (and rightly so) in a variety of ways not finally reducible to a set of "programs" taking place only within the local church. Well-received on the West Coast, the conversation begun there continued as we returned to Chicago and has been expanded to include chaplains, hospital personnel, child advocates, educators, and those who formulate public policy related to young children and their families.

And so we arrived at the present manuscript, understood by us to be a small but we hope a significant contribution in what we have come to perceive as a much needed, ongoing conversation about the church's ministry with young children. We believe church leaders will be able to use this book as a springboard into an ongoing discussion—with teachers, nurses, legislators, chaplains, parents, and others who are intentionally involved in the lives of children.

We want to thank those persons whose critical comments along the way have helped us—Margaret B. McFarland, Charlotte Collier, Mary Anne Fowlkes, Judy Hill, Karen Maurer, Jo Bennett Mitchell, and Donald Richter. We also want to thank those peers in ministry who allowed us to use their "stories"—Audrey Witzman, Fran Tellner, David Owens, Marcia Heeter, Yvonne White Morey, Don Griggs, and Patricia Griggs. In addition, the competence and caring concern of our editors, Barbara Withers and Susan C. Winslow, have carried us through the rough spots. And finally, a special note of thanks to our own children, now young adults—Michal, Melissanne, and Jason. They are in this book; in many respects, it is *their* book.

INTRODUCTION

Concern for children is virtually universal. (Only a few people, such as the late humorist W. C. Fields, profess a dislike or disdain for children!) We once were children ourselves, and many of us are responsible, as parents, care givers, teachers, or extended family, for the welfare of children. Our interest and concern may be direct and immediate—caring for one or more children in our own home, classroom, or care unit. Or it may be broad and far ranging—wanting children to receive our tradition and preparing them to fulfill our future. We know that the welfare of the human race and human community depends on helping children become the very healthiest, most mature, and most capable persons they possibly can be. Instinctively we sense our share in the tasks of helping our children to grow into mature, responsible human beings.

Most of us have experienced joy in our relationships with children. The rewards for being with them have been deeply satisfying, making worthwhile whatever pains or inconveniences it costs to feed, clothe, teach, and guide them. Not that we are perfect parents, teachers, counselors, or healers. After all, children are not mechanical toys that can be wound up and made to behave just so. They are human and will express their freedom; and in the end, that is what we want for them. Nevertheless, even if previous generations could claim that social conditions made it difficult to raise children, the present generation of adults is experiencing peculiar horrors that frighten us and devastate our children. Poverty, violence, abuses of all sorts, and dysfunctions of family and community harden our children. In some places hunger and preventable disease or outright war kill our children. Contorted values that drive us to spend and accumulate or to alienate and isolate, mold our children into distorted and warped personalities that are incapable of loving and serving others or truly enjoying the gifts of creation. Being a child today is not easy; we know it, and we seek guidance as we try our best to prepare our children to live in this real world. We hope that we can instill in our children positive values that will motivate them to change the world we are asking them to inherit and inhabit.

Religious education books of the last several generations have been useful. They have provided us with insights from Jean Piaget on how children think or from John Dewey on how children learn. Many other wise scholars and teachers have been influential. These books have been sympathetic to children, eliciting from us the need to sympathize with how children think, how they talk, how they see the world through young eyes experiencing things for the first time. The better books have also been empathetic, revealing the actual language and art of children, so that we adults could begin to recall or grasp how children feel and what they really need, rather than what we adults determine they need.

Now Barbara and Bill Myers have given us this book about children that is not only sympathetic and empathetic but also prophetic and empowering. *Engaging in Transcendence: The Church's Ministry and Covenant with Young Chil-*

dren tells the story of children with profundity and artistry. We are called to act justly toward our children and to empower them to fulfill the promise of mature personhood and fruitful membership in community.

In the first chapter we are enabled to recall or to see for the first time what it is like to be a young child who is learning by touching, tasting, exploring, and even by sloshing in mud puddles. With genuine sympathy the Myerses impute significance to the natural activities the young child experiences. The child learns from even the smallest acts of ordinary living with ordinary people like us. We are excited by the sacredness of the ordinary, for there is where God fosters the child's growth. We are motivated to honor the ordinary and to experience alongside the child the joy and excitement of learning by living.

As the young child reaches out, taking steps for the first time, trying to overcome a hurdle or to put thoughts together in new combinations, the child is transcending, or going beyond, current limits and stretching toward God's whole creation. It is becoming more and more fully the self God intended this child to be. In chapter 2 we adults are called to be trustworthy and to offer young children a world that is trustworthy. We offer a world characterized by hope. Thus a child is willing to venture forth, to try new things, not fearing failure or feeling despair.

God is trustworthy and promises every child the possibility of growing into maturity. Adults and the world are not perfect, however, nor are children forever innocent. We all make mistakes, and we get caught up in hurtful situations. Now the child must learn that hurt can be overcome, and relationship and hope can be restored. Reconciliation occurs and is learned by participation in loving communities. The family needs to be such a community. So does the community of faith. Chapter 3 shows that the church, in its various forms such as the nursery school or day-care center, is part of the loving environment in which caring people help children to deal with relationships that have been broken or identities that have been threatened. Children and parents alike can experience and can learn from the community of faith how to be in loving, forgiving, and accepting relationship. Caring adults can relate with children so as to affirm them and confirm their sense of identity and selfhood.

Chapter 4 recognizes the importance of helping organizations such as hospitals. Children cannot be completely shielded from sickness or even death. They experience trauma. Their own bodies are hurt, or they see the pain experienced by people close to them. Social workers, nurses, doctors, counselors, teachers, and numerous others have a ministry with children if they will. These people, through their jobs—their callings—can be partners with parents, families, and congregations as they help children.

Children seem to grow best when four conditions are met: acceptance of context, caring presence, hospitality, and transcendence. By naming and describing these basic conditions the authors help us to shape an effective ministry with children. Thus one hunch is confirmed—working with children is much more than teaching them Bible stories in a Sunday church school classroom. Children's ministry is comprehensive and heavily weighted toward relationships and activities in which people interact and incarnate love and acceptance.

Indeed the traditional Sunday school is overloaded with "hidden curriculum." Wittingly or not, many Sunday schools push upon the children dubious cultural values and moralisms. Grace is contradicted. The required lessons often inhibit children from making grateful response to God's gift of salvation and God's call into community and discipleship. The Bible story is often told poorly and comes across as nice sentiments or rigid demands. Chapter 5 suggests that the primary agency for communicating the faith is the congregation. The Sunday church school is but one of many valuable educational strategies for nurturing children in the faith and preparing them for maturity and mission. Participating in the full range of congregational worship, fellowship, study, and service, children experience and reflect on how to be a Christian and a member of God's community of faith.

Worship, particularly, is a congregational activity that needs to be seen in a radically different way. This is the message of chapter 6. Children come to worship not primarily to learn some things about God and how we pay respect to God. Rather, children are themselves worshipers, who like other worshipers praise God, seek God's forgiveness and restoration of relationship, and receive God's Word through the sacraments and preaching. Children are children, so worship needs to be conducted so as to be relevant to their interests and abilities. Anyone of any age would desire content and processes in worship that are understandable and practical. And the presence of children in worship is important for the children themselves and for the other worshipers too. Children practice and proclaim faith and share love and joy during worship. They express trust and can encourage others to be trusting. Their presence fulfills the congregation's being as a worshiping household of God.

The power of chapter 7 lies in the naming of the abuses that children endure in the "toxic cultures" of the present day and more so in the examples of how children have survived the toxins. Working within the environment of context, presence, hospitality, and transcendence, "ritual elders" have helped children to overcome various "toxic cultures," be they in the comfortable suburb of Winnetka or the harsh war zone of Solentiname in Nicaragua. Using the resources of faith and love, adults have accompanied children on their journey toward creative, wholesome life. This chapter tells us, who care very much about children, that "it can be done."

Chapter 8 affirms ministry with children within the community of faith and calls for ministry to children who are not members of the worshiping community. Children are recipients of ministry, but they are not targets of a ministry aimed at conversion. Children possess intrinsic value and integrity. Indeed, even as we minister with children in the congregation, they as children minister to us. They also can be ministers to other children outside the walls of the church. This final chapter reminds us of the church's mission to nurture its members—including children—and to teach them and prepare them for ministry and then send them into the world to live life and perform ministry.

The church's ministry with children *is* covenantal, as the title of this book suggests. The people of God promise to be present with the children, in a hospitable context in which children can experience the transcendence that brings them to the holy place where every child is known by name and is loved and accepted as a person. That holy place every child enters is the realm of God.

DAVID NG
San Francisco Theological Seminary

CHAPTER ONE

BURNING BUSHES
THE PRIMACY OF EXPERIENCE

> *Earth's crammed with heaven,*
> *And every common bush afire with God;*
> *But only he who sees takes off his shoes;*
> *The rest sit round it and pluck blackberries.*
> —ELIZABETH BARRETT BROWNING, "AFIRE"

Roy Larson, former religion writer for the *Chicago Sun-Times*, once mentioned that, like a wistful character from a John Updike novel, he kept examining the world for the fingerprints of God. Quoting Abraham Heschel, Larson went on to say that he believed he was more likely to find God's fingerprints on a kitchen table than on a holy altar. "Supernatural splendor," Heschel said, emanates "from ordinary acts." The place to look for "spiritual substance," he insisted, "is in everyday existence." Even the most simple deeds can be "full of wonder."

Reading Heschel again, the authors are reminded of the rabbi who was once asked why no one nowadays sees God. The sage replied that people are not willing to look that low. The fingerprints of God are not all that difficult to spot—once you've found the proper angle of vision.

AN ANGLE OF VISION

When the authors' older daughter was two years old, the distance from our small apartment on Adrian Avenue to Joe's grocery three blocks away could be covered in a few minutes. But when Michal walked with us, the three blocks were filled with curbs to step up and down several times over, and rocks had the most interesting things crawling underneath them. People of all sizes invited watching. Four-legged creatures passed by at different distances and in different ways. Sometimes there were puddles, sometimes leaves to crunch or gravel to sort though. Walking to Joe's took more than a few minutes, and we parents saw things we had not seen for a long time. When we were open to Michal's "angle of vision," rich memories stirred inside us of awe and of hands that once held our own. Michal helped us reawaken the feelings, experiencing dimensions of the child often hidden deep within us.

Poets and artists can also help us as adults to reconnect and to adjust our angle of vision. For example, Georgia O'Keeffe, an artist known for her distinctive use of form and color, who died in 1986, continues to encourage us to see the powerful forces of the ordinary. Her bleached bones, shells, and New Mexico landscapes have become icons in American art. She expressed her ideas in relation to her work in *Pelvis Series—Red with Yellow*:

> When I started painting the pelvis bones I was most interested in the holes in the bones—what I saw through them—particularly the blue from holding them up in the sun against the sky as one is apt to do when one seems to have more sky than earth in one's world. . . . They were most wonderful against the Blue—that Blue will always be there as it is now after all man's [sic] destruction is finished.[1]

The place to look for "spiritual substance," insisted Heschel, "is in everyday existence." Even the most simple moment—to look at blue sky through a hole in a bleached, white bone—can be filled with wonder.

THE ORIGINAL VISION

As persons concerned with the "religious," we would do well to remember that children, artists, and poets minister to us whenever they provide us with "angles of vision" into this world that help us reconnect with the experience that feeds the imagination of the child still residing within our adult bodies. In research done by Edward Robinson, adults who were asked to recall their religious experience often reflected upon the special sense of the world they once possessed as children but had lost in adulthood. In his book *The Original Vision*, one of Robinson's respondents recalled a moment as a young child spent walking on the moors. As a child, this person "knew that I had my own special place, as had all other things, animate and so-called inanimate, and that we were all part of this universal tissue which was both fragile yet immensely strong and utterly good and benefi-cent." Reflecting on the power of this moment, this person was convinced that "the vision has never left me. It is as clear today as fifty years ago, and with it the same intense feeling of love of the world and the certainty of ultimate good." As an adult, this person affirmed that "the whole of this [childhood] experience has ever since formed a kind of reservoir of strength from an unseen force."[2] Such child-hood memories are the imaginative building blocks of adult faith. Such memories provide lifelong images of how the world "is" for "me." These images are precursors to what we, as adults, later name as "faith."

Robinson notes that adults often recall such childhood memories as if they occurred yesterday, relying on them for more or less hopeful interpretations of their adult worlds. Thus one of Robinson's adult respondents wrote: "When I was about five I had an experience on which, in a sense, my life has been based. . . . Every single person was a part of a Body." Robinson's fascination with this respondent con-

tinued, even as the respondent puzzled over the importance
and the underlying meaning conveyed by such a seemingly
bizarre image. The respondent believed that "this inner
knowledge was exciting and absorbingly interesting, but it
remained unsaid because, even if I could have explained it,
no one would have understood. Once, when I tried, I was
told I was morbid."[3] Unfortunately, the powerful image
experienced by this child was never affirmed, discussed, or
listened to by adults.

When we engage, as adults, in faith explorations, sometimes we go back to such unnamed experiences and feelings
from our earliest years, back to the raw knowing that
precedes and undergirds our words and symbols, back to
what Douglas Sloan terms "participatory knowing."[4] Such
"knowing," as Sloan suggests, "takes place in a participation, an immersion in the very being of the world in which
we are living."[5] Because, as children, we were immersed in
certain experiences, now, as adults, we *know* certain things.
No one else knows what we know in exactly the same way
we know it. We know more than we can say. This "knowing" cannot be taken from us because, as children, we
embraced and participated in those experiential invitations
issuing from the unique world of our context. Sloan
stresses that such deep knowing "comes through activity."
Such knowing emerges from an active encounter that continues to inform the child over the course of her life; that is,
it is this "participatory knowing"—with all its communal,
experiential, contextual, and "immersive" aspects—that
lies at the base of the cognitive, interpretive, faithing
process of children and adults.[6] While Michal, for example,
cannot recall the specifics of what happened when she was
two years old and walked with us to Joe's grocery store, her
responsive engagement with us and with "the very being"
of the puddles, animals, leaves, and rocks discovered along
the way is what Sloan means by such "active knowing."

Adults who are in contact with young children like Michal continuously structure and extend despairing or hope-filled invitations to the child from the world in which the child is living. Thus, caring and responsive adults intentionally support the child's "active knowing" when they go walking with two-year-olds or help provide safe places where they can walk. And, if puddles are for splashing, adults who participate with young children on such walks might occasionally jump in!

THE BONDING PROCESS

In his book *Acquiring Our Image of God*, Martin Lang suggests that the "religious" in the life of a young child has its beginnings in the parent-child bonding process, a process that begins in the womb, where "the total complexus of symbols that constitutes the mother interacts intimately with the total complexus of systems that is the child."[7] Lang echoes Erik Erikson's assessment that trustful parent-child interactions are a "precondition for later religious appreciation."[8] Such positive bonding is connected within the meaning of the parents' life. Children are *immersed* in this parental understanding of the world. Lang, by stressing parent-child bonding, emphasizes the organic continuity of meaning between the mother and the child: "The mother knows the history of this relationship literally from its inception. The child's sense of meaning flows out of the biological and psychological rhythms of the mother. Meaning for the infant starts within and continues without, through being tended and touched."[9]

From before birth, the infant is immersed within the context of the family. Whatever the family constellation, these are the adults who initially mediate the world to the very young child. When the authors use the word family, we agree with Eugenia Hepworth Berger, who states that while "families in the United States and around the world are living with change, . . . the *essence* of the family remains stable with members of the family sharing a certain amount of commitment and support for each other." Berger holds that "the family is the most stable component of society." Thus, while the *form* may change, the family is that structure which interprets the world to its members: "If there is a bond among its members, with young children receiving necessary nurturing as well as shelter and food, then the family will survive."[10] The family, it is hoped, will thrive. In any case, the adults composing the family into which a child is born become the child's initial reference group as he or she compares and evaluates behaviors. Thus a child's caring adults help construct, with the child, a social reality within which family members live. This social reality is composed of the many experiences extended and interpreted by the family to the young child. And as the child responds to the contextual experiences in which he or she is immersed—we should recognize that such "participatory knowing" undergirds the grown adult's much later effort to abstract a "faith stance."

In Walter Brueggemann's words, as members of such "families," caring adults "practice a peculiar vocation," the creation of a "communal network of memory and hope in which individual members may locate themselves and discern their identities."[11] Thus, identity has a cultural location; experience is never neutral. Experience is always the extended invitation of the world—the cultural context mediated by the family—surrounding the child. Such "worlds" have value stances; none is value free. While the implications of these values often are not at the level of consciousness on the part of those adults within a child's context, they nevertheless provide value-laden invitations to the child. This "communal network of memory and hope," while part of the larger culture, has a story all its own. Occasionally we embellish these stories, imagining additions and interpretations, but then, "literal truth was never the point. What all these stories did was give us something strong and important to hold onto for as long as we needed it—a sense of belonging in the world."[12]

In this way, as a family practices its "peculiar vocation," children begin to understand their "own" angle of vision within the world and what it means to them. Every family story carries explicit and implicit messages about how the family relates to the big world. The authors' family remembers, for example, the courage of a young woman who, at age sixteen, left home to make her way in the world with all her belongings packed in a small paper bag. In retelling this story, that woman's daughter, now herself a parent, underscores her respect for her mother's courage and venturesome spirit. Such stories, owned and valued by a "communal network of memory and hope," powerfully frame the emerging "angles of vision" of our children.

A LARGER FAMILY—THE CHURCH

Just as families have stories, so do those institutions that are central in the lives of the family. In some forms of the Christian tradition, infants are baptized as part of the gathered congregation's common worship. Through this process children are named as members of a community that shares a common faith. Through the ritual of baptism, church members accept responsibility to become the spiritual godparents of the child so that as the child grows, he or she will do so within the faith story of the Christian community. Thus as the infant becomes the toddler and grows into the preschool and primary school years, the young child's world (his or her "story") continues to expand. To the degree that there is caring adult-child interaction, this expansion becomes a shared story, in fact a mutual learning process, a "participatory knowing," or what Erik Erikson terms "cogwheeling"; that is, the infant affects both church and parents, moving them along in their understandings, even as those same adults (and congregations) move the infant along in the infant's understandings.[13] Such mutual growth, or "cogwheeling," is a "school for learning" about the larger story, the mystery within which we (adults, congregations, and children) live.

Those churches and families within which Christianity most powerfully plays a key role educate their children when they actively bear that religious tradition into the participatory *experience* of everyday living. Bonded to this family community, the young child becomes an active participant within meaningful activities. Unfortunately, often we (church congregation and family of origin) miss this point and attempt to transmit to the child more information than the child can understand. For example, as the authors' children moved out into the world, we found ourselves as a family engaged in a lot of "walks," that is, moments spent walking and being engaged by whatever the world had to offer us. On one occasion we walked along an ocean beach after a particularly hard rain. As adults, we were interested in what had washed ashore. Two-year-old Michal picked up a stick and dragged it after her. We could see that the ocean looked inviting; cool, clear, yet foamy. The problem that we faced was that we were blocked from access to that water by a marina fence that kept us on dry land. Michal, however, had told us that she wanted to throw her stick into the water, so we walked and walked and walked to come to the end of the marina fence. As adults, we knew eventually we would reach the ocean water, but Michal, having dragged her stick in an endless hike, suddenly ran to a rather common mud puddle and contentedly tossed her stick into the water! Later, as we considered what had occurred, it struck us that we had wanted to give Michal an ocean when a puddle was sufficient.

THE LANGUAGE OF FAITH: MUD-PUDDLE EXPERIENCE

Often we want to "give the ocean" to young children when splashing in a "puddle" is enough. We fall into this trap by the ways we choose to share our adult faith with our youngest children. In our hurry to communicate our faith, we often assume that words are the most effective vehicle. Yet by using only words, we may fail to engage children in those common mud-puddle experiences where God is most visible, such as sitting on a loved person's lap and hearing a story, helping to bake bread, sharing a doughnut, or going with someone for a walk. These are the simple ways by which adults nurture and tend to the religious experience of children.

The institutional church, unfortunately, often overlooks such participatory experience and substitutes a canned curriculum for such common, ordinary happenings. "Canned curriculum" here means a printed, generic curriculum that assumes *anyone* can use it. The question then becomes, Who can "fill the slots" to "teach the curriculum"? Such an approach often avoids the necessity of providing ongoing relationships and does not promote experiential interaction on the basis of the adult's familiarity with and understanding of a child's world. It therefore came as no surprise to the authors that over a quarter of Robinson's younger respondents in *The Original Vision* reported that after enduring the church's labored efforts, as adults they ultimately rejected organized religion. In a telling passage, Robinson ponders this substantial minority:

Religion may be accepted when it offers a language,
a means of interpretation, for an awareness of some-

thing already sensed, however dimly, to be real; but when it is seen merely to be presenting ready-made solutions—no. "There seemed nothing in the church that bore any correspondence *with my own experience.*" That alone, it is implied, is real; that alone is authentic [italics added].[14]

Persons necessarily use words in talking about their religious feelings and experiences. Pooling their individual stories, groups (usually, until the late twentieth century, composed primarily of men) have authored creeds, formulas, and dogmas. As a result, religions, or what James Fowler calls "cumulative traditions," often seem to be dominated by words.[15] It is of interest that Fowler (among others) uses "cumulative traditions" to describe religion. While such a phrase need not be negative, it does suggest something about the way a person's faith (initially triggered by certain experiences) becomes institutionalized. The church then becomes the repository of the "old" experience, a conservator that tends to be suspicious of any "new" experience. Fowler notes, however, that a lively faith is possible only as such cumulative traditions are open and encouraging to the dynamic that gave birth to them. Once those within the cumulative tradition (say, Roman Catholic, Russian Orthodox, Lutheran, United Presbyterian, or United Church of Christ) forget how to see, feel, touch, taste, or smell the experiences that sparked the cumulative tradition in the first place, the traditions become destructive to faith.[16] The child benefits from such "cumulative traditions" only when such religions provide experiences appropriate to a child's participation.

Such an observation is not new with the authors. Writing in 1932, John Dewey made a distinction between the term religious and the term religion.[17] For Dewey, "religion" was the formal expression (words, symbols, dogmas) that evolved out of specific cumulative traditions. In contrast, the "religious" was that "quality of experience" underlying the words, symbols, and dogmas of particular religions.[18] While Dewey was not writing for the church, those of us who are concerned for the church should recognize that calcified cumulative traditions can be viewed as impediments distancing children from God. People caught in static cumulative traditions often seem to study abstractions and creeds instead of responding to the reality of their lives. When "religion" in this static sense is more honored than experience, Dewey suggests, the "religious" dies.

RECONNECTING

What ought adults who work in and around religious institutions do about those young children in their midst? An initial step would be to sort out the ways in which adults and children are similar and different. As adults we share common feelings with children—joy, anger, fear, and confusion. Yet, we are different; for while we share common feelings, we *think* about things differently. The way we tend to think often cuts us off not only from the intensity of our feelings but also from the more open, imaginative, childlike side of adulthood. If childhood can be understood to be a dimension of all of life rather than one chronological moment in a life, then when persons cut themselves off from this dimension, they tend to be less receptive of religious experience. Adults seem to cut themselves off from imaginative childhood with regularity. It should not be surprising that religious educators such as Maria Harris and Craig Dykstra suggest that those concerned with the "religious" should pay more attention to experience, imagination, and vision.[19] This simple observation may be a profound one when we consider ways in which children often *minister* to adults! (For more on this see chapter 6.)

Although children have a more imaginative picture of the world than adults have, children haven't been around as long. Their reservoir of experience is only two, three, four, or five years deep. One place this becomes evident is in children's art. In the introduction to Nancy Smith's book *Experience and Art*, Elliot W. Eisner shares a basic understanding underlying effective work with young children—"The character of the images children make is directly related to the quality of thinking they are able to employ."[20] Smith then describes ways two-year-olds and young threes make marks with their crayons that are basically records of their movements. Through their motor interactions with crayons, pencils, markers, and paint, they discover that crayons and pencils make lines and that paint can become dots and splashes. Then children begin to *control* their scribbles and to make their art tools do what the children want. Lines can curve or be straight or go up and down. As they grow, experience, experiment, explore, work, and play, they figure out that the marks they make can represent people, members of their family, friends, houses, and cars. Then the marks become representations or symbols of human experience. At first the symbols vary—one minute the human figure may be made in a certain way; ten minutes later it may be drawn entirely different. But as children continue to grow, work, experience, explore, and play, their symbols become more clearly defined and consistently representative of specific images. In this process they learn culturally shared symbols.

It is easy for us to understand such a complex process when we picture how it works in relation to concrete objects, for example, the experiences that make up the concept of apple. Through interactions with others who use the term apple, children come to know the essence of (and later become able to talk, read, and write about) what in the English language is termed "apple." For adults, the simple act of reading the word apple can bring up memories of all kinds of past experiences with apples. While our own personal experiences form our own unique mental images of "apple," we share a common verbal and written symbol when we talk and write about apples. This is true of all symbols, for example, a candle burning on an altar, a wreath on a door, a turkey on a Thanksgiving Day table, a star over a crèche at Christmastime. It is also true of the spoken and written word "God."

As children continue to grow, explore, and play, their symbols become more clearly defined and more consistently representative of specific images. In this way they are immersed in and come to know and name their participatory experience, even as they imaginatively move into what Fowler has called "the force field of life."[21] A faith that allows us, and our children, to move into "the force field of life" is more than verbal creeds and dogma; it is dynamic, alive, vibrant.

As a community of persons sharing a living faith tradition, the church provides time, space, and concrete experiences through which children gradually come to know the words and other symbols that represent the faith of their parents. In this process, creeds, dogmas, music, and rituals representing the parents' heart-held beliefs take on renewed meaning for both generations but only when experiences within the church community are congruent with the essence of the dynamic faith that gave birth to the words and other symbols in the first place. In her beautiful book *3's in the Christian Community*, Phoebe Anderson provides rich resources for those adults who teach and care for young children in the Sunday church school. Her book is a clear example of the powerful and positive role teachers have within this process. Recognizing, valuing, and supporting members of the faith community charged with responsibility for this Sunday program is essential, yet all church communities share an even broader challenge. The *religious* education of the young cannot occur solely within a weekly one-hour format.[22]

VOCATION—OUR CALLING

Walter Brueggemann frames the problem for us when he comments about our vocation as "calling" (*vocatio*, "call"). We are *called*, Brueggemann is saying, *called* into "the creation of a communal network of memory and hope."[23] To be "called" implies that God has an interest in this process. God is the transcendent reference point for who we are and what we do. We are called into relationships. We have, in the Judeo-Christian tradition, a rich model for this relationship. We call this relational way of understanding and being in the world *covenant*. A God of love stands with us in this world and expects us to remember and then create out of that memory an ongoing "communal network of memory and hope." To create implies that we move into the unknown, experiencing all the terrors and joys connected with the unsettling process of transcending what has become comfortable and, in some sense, rigid. To remember implies recalling the rich stories, traditions, and experiences that have informed our community of saints. Remembering suggests storytelling, cross-generational communication, common experiences informed through shared worship and engagement in our world. To hope implies a vision emerging from a trustworthy grounding. Hoping rests, after all, in the certainty that there is an openness to the future.

Remembering Brueggemann's claim that caring adults need to create a "communal network of memory and hope in which individual members may locate themselves and discern their identities," adults who are concerned about the quality of life together will work at this process and pay attention to it.[24] The church also will actively engage, to use the words of historian Frank E. Reynolds, in the "cultivation of Christian worlds."[25] Both Brueggemann and Reynolds are clear—teachers, other adults, families, and religious leaders must intentionally nurture and shape alternative forms of social reality, practicing those forms in compelling ways designed to permit, encourage, and authorize children to function "*in tension with* the technically-constructed, bureaucratically-ordered state, city or city state."[26] By such actions the family, caring adults, and the church counter what is taught by the culture through its bureaucratic mythology and ideology.

Many adults are aware that, for whatever reasons, the belief systems of the United States are often destructive to the health of the family and young children. The values of rampant individualism, competition, and a materialistic quest for success (regardless of what this might mean for others) flood the family. Sometimes adults accede to these values, becoming incapable of critical reflection. Some critics of our culture's current values suggest that such accommodation is a domestication process; that is, like young puppies, we are housebroken in order that we may fully participate in this culture. Brueggemann puts it like this: "Many of us are domesticated enough so that we understand the family to be a device to nurture folks so that they are suitable and effective participants in the dominant value system." But here he notes the radical power of the Bible in countering this experience: "To the extent that the family is to support and enhance the dominant system of technology and ideology, I submit no help can be found in the Bible."[27] According to Brueggemann, the interplay of religious and cultural values within this biblical-cultural tension results in the family playing a key role in the crucial moments "of hurt and amazement" in a child's life.[28] Such moments are profoundly educative and religious but only if caring, covenantal adults can name them from within a tradition that has vitality, credibility, and authority. (For more about this see chapters 6, 7, and 8.)

Let the authors step back, for a moment, and summarize the argument. We have suggested that active, lively, participatory experiences within which consistently caring adults and young children are immersed provide young children with positive building blocks. Later, as adults, they will come to construct from such building blocks their own interpretive understanding of faith. In this process, adults provide young children with invitations to the world-shaping dimensions of faith or hold them back. Often these messages emerge through the normal, ongoing life patterns associated with families and faith traditions. The experience of the child is profoundly intertwined by the often unintentional consequences associated with belonging to a particular family or community of faith. But adults can be intentional about this process, as well as imaginative. We should not forget that the *community*, in tandem with the *family*, is a powerful presence in the developing lives of young children. People who believe ought to be developing communities of faith that are open and affirming to children and the wide variety of family constellations occurring in present-day American society. Invitations of faith will emerge in the practices of such communities.

For example, Patricia Polacco, the author of the children's book *The Keeping Quilt*, powerfully demonstrates the role played by that quilt in the creation of a "communal network of memory and hope." Told in a first-person narrative, *The Keeping Quilt* begins with memories about Great Gramma Anna, a Russian dirt-farmer's daughter who had come, with her family, to New York City. "The only things she had left of back-home Russia were her dress and the babushka she liked to throw up into the air when she was dancing."[29] As Anna grew, the babushka became the edge of a quilt, sewn by all the neighborhood ladies, so that the family would "always remember home."[30] The Friday night meal that initiated the Jewish Sabbath was served on this quilt, and Anna and Great-Grandfather Saska were married under the quilt as it became their wedding huppa. Later,

> when my Grandma Carle was born, Anna wrapped her daughter in the quilt to welcome her warmly into the world. Carle was given a gift of gold, flower, salt, and bread. Gold so she would never know poverty, a flower so she would always know love, salt so her life would always have flavor, and bread so she would never know hunger.[31]

Carle married Grandpa George under the quilt, danced with members of the community at the wedding, and also received the same gifts as at her birth. They moved to a farm in Michigan; Carle gave birth to Mary Ellen, who also was wrapped—for warmth—in the quilt. Anna, now called "Lady Gramma," came to live with them. She wrapped her legs in the quilt to keep warm, and celebrated her ninety-eighth birthday with a cake. The cake rested on the center of the quilt.

When Anna died, the storyteller Patricia Polacco relates, "My mother Mary Ellen was now grown up."[32] Mary Ellen married, also under the quilt, and received gold, bread, and salt in her wedding bouquet. Eventually, the quilt "welcomed me, Patricia, into the world . . . and it was the tablecloth for my first birthday party."[33] Sometimes the quilt became a play-tent; at other times it rested on Patricia's bed. When Patricia married, the wedding ceremony was under the quilt, and she also carried flowers, gold, bread, salt, "and a sprinkle of wine, so I would always know laughter."[34] *The Keeping Quilt* ends: "Twenty years ago I held Traci Denise in the quilt for the first time. Sometime she, too, will leave home and she will take the quilt with her."[35]

In *The Keeping Quilt*, simple pen-and-ink drawings dominate, except for a concentrated splash of colors—the treasured quilt—as it appears on every page. The multihued quilt stands out in the midst of common, ordinary, everyday happenings. Indeed this quilt, sewn together from scraps of Great Gramma's dress, "Uncle Vladimir's shirt, Aunt Havalah's nightdress, and an apron of Aunt Natasha's,"[36] embodies one example of a family's "communal network of memory and hope." Like the poem by Elizabeth Barrett Browning that opened this chapter, *The Keeping Quilt* suggests that all of earth is "afire with God," if we have the proper "angle of vision."

CHAPTER TWO

HERE BE DRAGONS

A CURRICULUM OF TRANSCENDENCE

"Here be dragons." Whenever ancient mapmakers came to the end of known land, they would inscribe this legend on their maps: "Here be dragons." This inscription meant that here was the unknown. And what happened when someone sailed into the unknown? No one knew for sure. Perhaps sailors were drowned; perhaps, just perhaps, people were devoured by dragons.

There are many matters related to children and the church—"dragons" from the deep—that should be of concern to us. But of deepest concern for all of us is "the development of a sense of faith that invites and permits children and parents and all adults to learn and to hope—to lean and move with expectancy into our future."[1] It is this kind of open and hope-filled faith, as Erik Erikson and others tell us, that we as Christians believe should pervade the way in which we educate and care for our young. At best, such a trusting yet realistic faith involves a spirited confidence in our own understandings—our own story or tradition—and a sense of hope that things can be better. But how do young children arrive at such hope and confidence? We believe that the dynamic of transcendence undergirds all our interactions with experience, and the degree to which persons successfully participate in experience marks how we come to know ourselves as being spirited, hopeful, and able to learn, persons marked by confidence instead of fear. Perhaps we can best understand the dynamics of transcendence by watching a young child as she tries to stand and walk.

TRANSCENDENCE

Grabbing a table leg, the authors' ten-month-old Melissanne determinedly pulls herself upright. Both her legs are shaking, but she won't allow herself to slip back onto the floor. Supporting herself as she moves, hand over hand, around a corner of the tabletop, Melissanne conveys a sense of great seriousness, even as she looks toward her mother, who is seated at some distance from Melissanne's last available handhold. Chewing her lip, but keeping one hand upon the tabletop, Melissanne stretches toward her mother until, for the briefest of moments, she hesitantly stands alone. Tumbling down, Melissanne chortles with glee, grabs the nearest table leg and once more pulls herself upright, ready to repeat the process.

Most human beings, like Melissanne, begin by crawling on this earth but soon learn how to stand upon both feet and reach for the stars. While Melissanne's encounter with the table leg emphasizes the positive aspects of human aspiration, the story of the Tower of Babel in the book of Genesis suggests the negative consequence of overreaching (Gen. 11). Human beings "created in the image of God" naturally reach for the stars, but only God, the Genesis story seems to say, limitlessly transcends all that is known. The word God names the *transcendent* one, and *transcendence* marks us as being created in God's image. Humans created in God's image may share in the ongoing dynamic of transcendence, Genesis suggests, but this is transcendence within the limits of our created nature. Nevertheless, when Melissanne stands, tumbles down, and chortles with glee, she intuitively senses that there is more to being human than crawling.

Bernard Lonergan, the late Canadian Jesuit theologian, anchored his theological method upon this intrinsic human dissatisfaction with what we have and who we are. Lonergan said that we "achieve authenticity in *self-transcendence* [italics added]."[2] His suggestion was that the desires and longings we have for what is beautiful, for what makes sense, for what is true, and for what has value are at the heart of what it means to be human. Recognizing that these longings and aspirations remain in the human heart even after every need seems to have been met, we might say that no state of being, no material thing, no explanation or system, ultimately satisfies us because we were made for more, for transcendence.

The word transcend comes from *transcendere*, which literally means "to climb over." The word transcendence points at the process of moving over, going beyond, across, or through real or imagined limits, obstacles, or boundaries. Lonergan urges us to befriend these inner desires of the heart for *transcendence* and to recognize the inner tugs they exert on us, even as they call us out of ourselves and into the world. In this process, he believes, such longings from the human heart are ultimately satisfied through a relationship with God.[3] But Melissanne, at ten months, isn't quite ready to *talk* about her experience and what it means (or doesn't mean) about God. She is engaged in *experiencing* transcendence as she pulls herself up into a whole new angle of vision.

Young children like Melissanne are continuously issued invitations by the context in which they live. Families, other adults, and communal institutions such as the church implicitly anchor such invitations within cultural and religious value systems. It is better to stand than to crawl. In this process one is rewarded by smiles and encouragement. As young children actively respond to such invitations, they are immersed in the process of moving over, going beyond, across, or through real or imagined limits, obstacles, or boundaries.

A CURRICULUM OF TRANSCENDENCE

Philip Phenix argues that the world, and ultimately, God, continues to engage every human being within just such a "curriculum of transcendence." He notes: "It is phenomenologically not the case that some persons, called 'religious' or 'spiritual' types, experience [transcendence] while others do not." In that *every* human experiences transcendence, Phenix is "arguing that human consciousness is rooted in transcendence, and that analysis of all human consciousness discloses the reality of transcendence as a fundamental presupposition of the human condition."[4]

When Phenix claims transcendence as "the inescapable reality of human existence," he defines the word transcendence as "the experience of limitless going beyond any given state or realization of being."[5] For Phenix, this possibility of "going beyond" means that the material certainties of "my life" as well as "who I am" are always open, never final, and continually exist within a context of ever wider relationships and possibilities. He suggests that a closer look at these things uncovers their impermanence; that is, nothing, including who we are, is "just what it appears to be here and now without any further prospects or associations."[6]

"Spirit" becomes the word that names the "property of limitless going beyond."[7] When a person like Melissanne is said to "have spirit," such a person expresses "perennial discontent and dissatisfaction with any and every finite realization."[8] In other words, "spirit" is that which enables Melissanne to "chortle with glee" when she tumbles down and begins again the process of pulling herself upright. By meeting life's invitations, Melissanne is engaged in a spirited, "never finished enlargement of contexts."[9] Transcendence engages children because, as Jerome Berryman suggests, "They live at the limit to their being and knowing most of the time."[10]

The ongoing dynamic of transcendence suggests a new understanding of "curriculum" for children. A curriculum in tune with transcendence cannot be purchased from the "canned" resources of a denominational publishing house. Denominational literature can inform the ways we plan for children, but this "curriculum of transcendence" emerges from the experience of life itself. For example, when adults require children to encounter new events like beginning preschool, accepting the arrival of a sibling, sustaining the absence of a loved one, going on a lengthy trip, or being in a hospital, these children are being involved in experiences of transcendence. Such experiences are transcendent not because they fit within certain categories of organized religion but because children have been asked to move beyond the known into the unknown. Such movement provokes questions such as, "Who is going to take care of me?" "Will I be all right here?" "Can I handle this new situation?" While such questions might be labeled, depending on who is doing the labeling, as either "developmental" or "religious," such questions are in fact indications of transcendence.

The beginning of this chapter recalled how, in ancient times, sailors who ventured beyond the known world feared that they might "fall off" and be devoured by dragons. "Here Be Dragons," the old mapmakers would inscribe. Children, moving out into the unknown world, face equally uncertain terrain. "Spirited" children set sail into their futures, and we who are adults greet them—

either as encouragers of the ongoing process of transcendence or as mean-spirited dragons, capable of destruction and death. Clearly children live on the edge, facing terrain that is uncertain. "Here Be Dragons"? Perhaps so.

LIVING ON THE EDGE

The well-known Harvard child psychiatrist and author Robert Coles interviews, observes, and writes about the lives of people on the edge, particularly children. When Coles lectures, he often tells the story of Ruby, a six-year-old whom he observed and interviewed when, as one of four African American children, she was a primary participant in the 1960 desegregation of two New Orleans public schools. "Here was a little girl who was called every name in the book, who was insulted and threatened, and yet could find time in the evening to pray for the people who were heckling her and could even pray for them while walking in their presence, while being insulted by them." Coles goes on to say that Ruby could do this "because Christ had told her something, namely that she must forgive these people because they didn't know what they were doing."[11] With wonder in his voice, Coles states that he has spent his life trying to understand how children like Ruby—whom he considers his "greatest teacher"—*transcend* their circumstances.[12] He reflects: "What can you say, psychiatrically, sociologically, in terms of developmental theory, as it's put, when you have a six-year-old child with that kind of attitude?"[13] Throwing up his hands, he exclaims, "All you can do is be in awe of her."[14] But then he moves one step further—"I've never noted Ruby to be confused, or children like her. She knew exactly what she was doing. She had Biblical sanction for that kind of courageous suffering."[15]

From Ruby and Coles we learn that the experience of

transcendence never occurs in a vacuum. We might have a hunch that both Melissanne (as she takes an initial step) and Ruby (as she faces a hostile crowd) have been immersed from early on within a loving, caring, supportive, and challenging environment. Whatever "dragons" they may face will be met in spirited battle.

The first chapter drew upon Walter Brueggemann's work in indicating that adults are called into a peculiar vocation. As he put it, adults who care about children must be intentional about creating and nurturing "communal networks of memory and hope" in which individuals (like Ruby and Melissanne) can locate themselves and begin to discern their identities. Different environments equip children with different tools, so that they can powerfully, hopefully, and spiritedly negotiate the invitations issued by life. The Judeo-Christian tradition anchors the experience of human transcendence within a covenantal understanding of God as transcendent reference point for all human experience. Because of this grounding, one of Ruby's tools is the Bible as shared within her faith community. She had, says Coles, "Biblical sanction for that kind of courageous suffering."[16] Again, people who are "spirited" rarely become so in a vacuum. Erik Erikson points out that, while abstract words and theoretical concepts are not the conscious questions of young children, they concretely experience faith through relationships within a community that shares a common perspective, ethos, or "faith."[17] Children come to know, in Erikson's words, "an inner population of remembered and anticipated sensations and images which are firmly correlated with the outer population of familiar and predictable things and persons."[18]

As young children grow and move from trustworthy bases farther into their world, they can then move forward from their experience and respond in appropriate ways. From the growth associated with such experience, they come to expect themselves to be able to function competently in that world. In Erikson's framework this expectation is called basic *trust* (basic in that it is not always conscious). When children develop such a sense of basic trust, they can *hope*. Erikson describes such hope as "the ontogenetic basis of faith...nourished by the adult faith which pervades patterns of care."[19]

Take a moment to recap the discussion thus far. This book has suggested that *transcendence* is the underlying human dynamic, and that *spirit* and *hope* name qualities associated with how persons engage in or are prevented from engaging in transcendence. It has suggested that God is the one who limitlessly transcends, and it has noted that adults can either encourage or block children as they engage in transcendence. It has also suggested that the act of transcending a condition, like Ruby transcending the condition of hate or Melissanne transcending the condition of crawling, never occurs within a vacuum. The communal context within which a child grows is tremendously important. The very act of transcending assumes the presence of some form of adult community. The values that such a community affirms affect children as they engage in their worlds through the underlying dynamic of transcendence. Erikson affirms how important basic trust and mistrust are for the young child, and such qualities are mediated to him or her by the surrounding adults and institutions. Such qualities occur through the child's "participatory knowing," that is, through a sustained interaction occurring experientially with adults and the surrounding world.

THE HUMAN FACE OF GOD

While "transcendence" is the name of the underlying dynamic of the human condition and describes how experience becomes the curriculum of early childhood, the word does not contain sufficient moral imperative to clarify what is "appropriate and good and right behavior" on the part of those adults who regularly interact with young children. "Transcendence," however, assumes the presence of a Transcendent Other, that is, God. For example, persons from the Judeo-Christian tradition understand that the interactions of transcendence should be grounded in love; that is, adults should incarnate a loving presence with young children. Thus, when Christians use the word incarnation, we know it carries profound implications for how we view life. God's incarnation, we claim, can be seen in the human form of Jesus, whom we call Christ. This human person is God enfleshed, embodied, or incarnated. The transcendent God enters history. This powerful idea implies that those who believe in God, if they choose to follow God and accept the descriptive term Christian, join with Jesus in a continuation of the values related to this incarnational process. The process of transcendence is anchored within this certainty. Not that we become God, but we become the human face of God. Someone enmeshed in the values espoused by the Judeo-Christian tradition can discover many places, in addition to Jesus, where incarnation suggests (and, in fact, demands) that human beings become the human face of God.

Consider Jacob. Jacob, that cunning, slippery fellow, stole his brother Esau's birthright and fled, knowing that if Esau ever caught him, Jacob would die (Gen. 27). Tucked away in a foreign land, Jacob made money and grew powerful, but he was unhappy. After many years, he journeyed home. And, on that journey, Jacob wrestled with God in an effort to "see" God, to "know" God; but God still would not allow Jacob to see him. Frustrated, and limping from wrestling with God, Jacob continued on his way home. He assumed Esau still wanted to kill him, so still smooth, still tricky, Jacob sent gifts ahead to Esau to ease his return. The gifts dispersed, messengers came back to Jacob with frightening words—Esau awaited him with four hundred armed men. Still Jacob headed home, toward Esau. Listen to these words from that story: "But Esau ran to meet him, and embraced him, and fell on his neck and kissed him, and they wept" (Gen. 33:4). And Jacob said, "[Esau,] truly to see your face is like seeing the face of God—since you have received me with such favor (Gen. 33:10)." To repeat: "Esau, to see your face, is to see the face of God."

Such narratives carry a powerful Judeo-Christian message for those who have ears to hear. Those who work with, care for, or parent young children enter the process of transcendence as the "human face of God"; by so doing, those who care for and nurture children *incarnate* God's presence. And sometimes, children incarnate God's presence for the adults who care for them. Incarnation works both ways. Unfortunately, those who abuse and damage children incarnate the demonic. On such occasions, transcendence is blocked. While adults who interact with children must set appropriate limits to the relationship, we assume such relationships should have the shape of ongoing, sustaining, positive, care-giving, covenantal presences. How young children are cared for and educated really matters. A toxic world filled with inappropriate relationships muddies the waters; instead of helping, it stands in the way of a child's being able to know God's grace—which, we believe, becomes embodied in a child's participatory experience of relationships with caring adults. Here, in such love-filled experience, is where children continue to grow in their ability to accept life's invitations in hope-filled ways. But when community is undervalued, when adults forget their story, when persons are asked to care for too many children, when persons do not have the necessary resources, skills, knowledge, or energy to care for or to educate and do not know where to gain them, the world can be a toxic place for children—a place where "dragons" become real and a place where an evolving self can be poisoned rather than nurtured. The process of transcendence and the Transcendent One (God) are mocked. Environments provided by parents and institutions such as schools, churches, and hospitals can also be toxic—when there are too many strangers or adults who impose values and require behaviors that a child cannot produce or that are inconsistent with or in opposition to those of his or her family.

Sorting this out is a difficult process. This book assumes that the reader is aware of, and understands the power of, the religious within such a process. The authors, however, stand firmly within a particular form of the religious—the Christian tradition—and by so doing utilize (like Ruby) the narrative stories of that tradition. In that tradition, God is our transcendent reference point for all of living; the process of transcendence is the way we spiritedly move forward with that tradition's support in hope toward our future.

LIVING THE COVENANT

A central affirmation of the Christian faith is that we are loved by a God who will not let us go. One of the parables often used in illustration of this point is the story of the prodigal son (Luke 15). A son leaves home. We don't know why. Perhaps he was bored, curious, rebellious, ready to try something new. He went far, far away from home. Whatever the reason he left, things didn't work out. The world was not good to the son—he was reduced to eating the slop fed to pigs. But it was there, far from home, that the prodigal came to himself and headed home. The scripture is pointed: he knew he had been out of line; he knew his father owed him nothing; he knew there was no self-serving speech he might try with his father; he knew there might not be a ready welcome on the other side of the door . . . and yet, he headed home! And we know what he expected to discover.

The gospel is peppered with surprises. Do we expect an employer to pay different wages according to the different lengths of time people have worked? Surprise! Everyone is paid the same amount (Matt. 20). Do we expect the religious leader or the respected businessman to help that fellow in the ditch? Surprise! These "pillars" of the community pass by the wounded man, and it is a despised Samaritan who provides the care (Luke 10). Does a son, far from home, expect his father to say, "I told you so . . . you're nothing but a failure . . . you can't come home?" Surprise! A waiting parent stands with outstretched arms, anticipating, hoping, and waiting for the son's return. Stories like this tell us about God's *covenant*.

A *covenant*, in biblical terms, is not the same as a *contract*. When I contract with someone, there is a fair exchange. I dig a ditch and am paid wages for that work according to a certain scale. If, however, I am unable to complete my side of the contract, the holder of the other side of the contract is under no obligation to assist or pay me. I can be rejected because I have not fulfilled my side.

This contractual arrangement is the elder son's understanding of his relationship with his father. The elder son fulfilled his part of the bargain—he worked hard and expected a certain payoff because he had fulfilled his part of what he believed was an implicit contract. Surprise! The father in this story does not act out of a "contract mentality" with his children. Here the father extends his arms in love. Ultimately, this story tells us, we are bonded to a God of love who will not let us go and who always waits, at the end of the road, with open arms. This is a core concept of Christianity; to be the church implies that we who are adults must be about the creating, building, and maintaining of a participatory, relational way of life with and for children that is grounded more in trust than mistrust, but it is a way of life that also helps identify and address areas of mistrust. Because we educate within this covenantal understanding, our teaching is partisan. We have a story to tell, a vision of how the world works, a collection of ideas that help us sort out right from wrong.

Because this is true, we believe the church not only has a covenantal role to play in providing institutions that involve children (such as sponsoring preschools, engaging in intergenerational worship, and having an intentional presence in hospitals) but also that the church should engage in interpretive and helpful covenantal relationships with parents. Parents, for example, play out the covenantal "human face of God" by the way they "hold on" to and "let go" of their children. This is a key part of the ongoing process of transcendence in children's experience. As parents, we ought to talk about and share common experiences in such areas. Love, as a concept, becomes incarnated in the covenantal parent-child relationship as it unfolds, and "holding on" and "letting go" play out the nature of the support adults offer as the child experiences such transcendence.

HOLDING ON AND LETTING GO

We know, for example, that although the child becomes physically separate from the mother at birth, it is not until about two-and-a-half years later that the child attains a sense of constancy in the primary love or loves of his or her life. Through the process of holding on and letting go, the child at an early age experiences transcendence and checks out what we are calling covenantal love. For example, the authors' older daughter, Michal, became so adept at inventing ways of playing peek-a-boo that her father called her "the tiny peek-a-boo-er." She would crawl, dragging a diaper, into her parent's lap. Sitting upright, she would drape the diaper over her head. After waiting for a few seconds, she would jerk the diaper away, shrieking with delight. As she continued to grow, much of her play would center upon placing her teddy bear in a clothes closet, banging the door shut, saying, "Bye, bye, bear," and then quickly opening the door again. Children play through those things that they personally experience—and what better way to picture the permanence of covenantal relationships than to put teddy bear in the closet, say "Bye, bye, bear," and then cause the bear to reappear!

If we pay attention to these curriculums of transcendence, we might note that Michal was working through some powerful areas of concern—When mom and dad leave, can I trust them to return? Will the covenant hold? Still later, one of her favorite games was to ask her mother for a key. After receiving the key, she would open the front door, toddle through the doorway, and slam the door behind her while saying, "I goin' bye, bye, Mommy." Holding her key, she would play at locking the door and then knock on it. If her knocking did not result in her mother's immediately opening the door, she would call, "I home, Mommy." We can see that Michal was playing through very real issues. In this process, transcendence becomes visible.

What happens when Mommy goes to work? We must be clear—since children do not have the abstracting capability of adults, they need consistent, covenantal object relations. For example, Margaret Mahler describes a lag between what the psychologist Jean Piaget terms "object permanence" (the understanding that objects continue to exist even when they are out of sight) and the understanding that the most important persons in our lives continue to love us, to care for us, to be angry with us, to be there for us even when they are out of sight.[20] Adults can understand the covenantal abstractions of such concepts; children cannot. Transcendence is not always easy. In this instance, children are often left metaphorically "at sea," and, who knows, "dragons" might pull them down under the waves and devour them!

Nevertheless, adults often must leave children. Of key concern is that those who care for the child in such an absence can be trusted. For example, when Michal was sixteen months old, both of us enjoyed an occasional time away from baby, while Meredith, a friend's daughter who was known by and who knew Michal, babysat. The third time Meredith arrived, our daughter began to chant, "No moy Meredith, no moy Meredith." She had figured out that when Meredith arrived, we left. Having heard Michal's chant, we would leave the house, walk around a nearby corner, wait a few moments, and then return to listen at the door to see how it was going. And when we did this, we were able to hear Michal and Meredith happily playing. Michal had made her complaint, but she was able to move beyond the pain of our leaving because she was within the safe care giving of familiar and trusted Meredith. The covenant held. One more occasion of transcendence had been negotiated (spiritedly and in hope).

In the language of this chapter, Michal's "covenant" was in place, adults were "incarnating" love and appropriately caring for her, even when (curriculum of "transcendence") those adults on occasion nudged her onto the "waters." When this occurred, Michal's experience was such that no "dragons" took over her life. She "transcended" such experiences with spirit, even as her trusted adults considered how best to hold on and let go.

Having named this process from within the Judeo-Christian tradition, we can also reflect on how we might describe the same experience in the psychological terms of child development. For example, Louise Kaplan, building on the work of Margaret Mahler, helps us understand that during the first two and a half years of life, the human being moves from (1) an initial undifferentiated state, within which the world, the mother, and the self exist as one; to (2) a second state, where the infant senses the rest of the world as becoming "other," and the mother and self as sharing a common boundary; to (3) a third phase, where the toddler-young preschooler gradually sees the self as separate from the other, becoming an individual—or a "myself."[21] As our daughter Melissanne, when she was two-and-a-half years old, used to say, "My do it *myself*"!

Whether discussing holding on and letting go within a Judeo-Christian or a developmental understanding, the authors are reminded of Margaret Wise Brown and Clement Hurd's excellent book *Goodnight Moon* (referred to at the beginning of chapter 7). *Goodnight Moon* shows a trustworthy universe and one little bunny's small corner of it.[22] We see Little Bunny in bed, ready to fall asleep. Little Bunny's room is filled with numerous objects, including "a quiet old lady who was whispering 'hush.'"[23] This is a bedtime story, with the focus placed on saying "Goodnight" to every object in Little Bunny's room: "Goodnight room; goodnight moon; goodnight cow-jumping-over-the-moon."[24] Each object has one entire page with its own illustration. The ending line is, "Goodnight stars; goodnight air; goodnight noises everywhere."[25] The author of this book understands that bedtime often is a scary moment for little bunnies, and a lot of traditional nursery rhymes and prayers ("If I should die before I wake, I pray the Lord my soul to take") do not seem to help. *Goodnight Moon* speaks to that anxiety. It is a kind of cosmic "peek-a-boo"; when *you* (Little Bunny) wake up, everything will be all right. You,

Little Bunny, will be supported and embraced by covenantal love. And we believe that within the presence of such love rests the initial glimpses of the covenantal God, the Transcendent One, who loves and who will not let us go.

THE RUNAWAY BUNNY

When Michal entered college, we parents stood *with* her, though at a distance. "Letting go" had entered a new covenantal phase, as had "holding on." Such holding on and letting go involved an occasional parental visit to the young adult's new space. One of these visits found Barbara and Michal in the college bookstore. In the poster section, Michal drew Barbara's attention to a "Runaway Bunny" poster. Another story by Margaret Wise Brown and Clement Hurd, *The Runaway Bunny*, gently affirms that wherever Little Bunny runs to, the mother will be there.[26] This conversation is depicted in a series of delightful drawings in which Little Bunny is hidden in a setting, but the mother bunny can also be seen to be present. For example, Little Bunny says, "I will be a bird and fly away from you." The mother bunny responds, "If you become a bird and fly away from me, I will be a tree that you can come home to."[27] We see, in the accompanying drawing, Little Bunny using its rabbit ears to fly, while the mother bunny is drawn in the green, leafy shape of a tree waiting to catch Little Bunny.

When Little Bunny has exhausted all running-away possibilities, there are these closing lines: "Shucks," said the bunny, "I might just as well stay where I am and be your little bunny." And so he did. "Have a carrot," said the mother bunny,and we have a final drawing of the two of them, safe in their rabbit warren, munching carrots.[28] The runaway bunny's world is presented as an appropriately trustworthy place in which a caring adult is present for the

runaway bunny. A covenantal relationship is firmly established and never broken. The mother bunny incarnates the
human face of God.

While a runaway bunny poster was not the sort of poster
Barbara had expected to find in Michal's college bookstore,
Michal enthusiastically indicated that "someday she'd like a
copy of that poster." Barbara purchased the poster. On
subsequent visits to Michal, we were warmed to see the
poster of the runaway bunny hanging over her bed.

CHAPTER THREE

ORIGINAL GRACE
PRESCHOOL AND THE ADULT'S CARING PRESENCE

In the cartoon strip "Calvin and Hobbes," Calvin is a little boy whose imagination frequently transports him and his stuffed tiger, Hobbes, into an amazing variety of fantasies. In considering the exploits of this pair, a reader is never really clear where make-believe ends and reality begins. We can be certain, however, that in each day's comic strip, Calvin's "id" will unleash itself.

One early morning, Calvin, unable to escape his mother's insistence that he go to school, angrily awaits the school bus: "I don't want to catch the bus. I don't want to go to school. I don't want to be here at all," says Calvin to himself. A deepening scowl on his face underscores his feelings: "I'm sick of everyone telling me what to do all the time! I hate my life! I hate everything! I wish I was *dead*!" Struck by the intensity of this thought, Calvin reconsiders: "Well, no, I don't. Not really." And then exclaims (with an even deeper scowl on his face), "I wish everyone *else* was dead."[1]

On another occasion, Calvin is standing in a field. All around him are snowpeople he has built. Stuffed tiger Hobbes says, "Wow, you've made a lot of snowmen today!" Calvin replies, "Yep. They're effigies. Each one represents someone I hate." Scowling angrily, Calvin continues: "When the sun comes out, I'll watch their features slowly melt down their dripping bodies until they're nothing but noses and eyes floating in pools of water." Looking at the assortment of figures gathered in the field, Hobbes whimsically comments, "I wasn't aware you even knew this many people." Calvin, deep within his anger, doesn't even catch Hobbes's comment; he continues, "The ones I *really* hate are small, so they'll go faster."[2] Had Calvin surfaced in the early days of New England, his behavior would have been attributed to a perverse and sinful nature. In that day and age it was clear, at rock bottom, that children were sinners who shared in the legacy of original sin.

SIN AND NURTURE

Thus far, this discussion has focused upon the importance of *experience*, appropriately and covenantly mediated by adults, as children grow within contextual settings. The covenantal intentions and practices adults bring to such experiences affect the way children come to faith. It has also been noted that children never grow in a vacuum; the values of the larger community within which a child grows are powerfully presented as covenantal invitations or dragonlike blocks to transcendence.

Given this scenario, it is unfair to transport a thoroughly modern "Calvin" back to the early seventeen hundreds and expect either him or a Puritan New Englander like Jonathan Edwards to understand each other. It is, however, exactly the jarring associated with bringing such two characters together that illustrates how the values, beliefs, concepts, and concerns held by a community affect the way a child comes to adulthood.

For example, Jonathan Edwards' sermon "Sinners in the

Hands of an Angry God" was intended for all people, including children.[3] For the eighteenth-century New Englander, sin was a grounding theme of existence, a condition originating with Adam and transmitted via sexual intercourse into succeeding generations. The end result of such Augustinian logic was that the church of Edwards' time had come to understand all children as sinners. Had the cartoon figure Calvin been around in that time, he clearly would have been an appropriate target for conversion. Children of Calvin's age, roughly six or seven and up, were understood to be sinners who, while not deserving redemption, could seek it through the grace of God. Conversion was the preferred method of the church in this process.[4] Calvin would have resisted all such attempts. One wonders what might have happened to Calvin had he actually lived during those early days.

The idea that children were to be viewed by the church as if they were sinners in the hands of an angry God was challenged by Horace Bushnell in 1847. Bushnell believed in original sin, but he thought that a relational approach to children was more effective than one centered upon conversion. Because of the ensuing controversy, his little treatise *Discourse on Christian Nurture* was published but quickly withdrawn by the Massachusetts Sabbath School Society.[5] Having accented Christian nurture, Bushnell argued that society, instead of focusing on conversion, ought to concentrate on bringing up children relationally so that they would *always* understand themselves as Christians. Bushnell struck a chord when he proclaimed:

> The child, after birth, is still within the matrix of the parental life, and will be more or less, for many years. And the parental life will be flowing into him [sic] all that timme, just as naturally, and by a law as truly organic, as when the sap of the trunk flows into a limb.[6]

Attacking conversion as "mischievous individualism," Bushnell presented Christian nurture as an intermeshing of the social power of church, state, school, and family.[7] He understood Christianity

> not as something that explodes violently within human experience but, rather, as a life into which one grows, even if by fits and starts. The image of God in this vision is less that of one who demands earth-shaking, urgent decisions than of a person who is gentle, accessible, and patient.[8]

MAINLINE ACCOMMODATIONS

As outlined in this brief description, Bushnell's approach is similar to what this book affirms as incarnating God's human face by immersing children in community experience. Indeed, many of today's parishes and congregations continue to ground their practices concerning children within similar forms of Christian nurture, even while distancing themselves from the excesses of conversion. This practice has worked, more or less, but the success of such a strategy currently is in question because historically it has been dependent upon religious leaders and congregations stating a clear covenantal understanding and playing dominant roles within their society. When a small New England town was 90 percent Protestant Christian, it was easy to speak clearly and forcefully about bringing children up as Christians. Once composed of the "movers and shakers" in the culture, these congregational clusters of Protestant Christians often drew the descriptive adjective of "mainline," or "mainstream."

The cultural dominance of these mainline Protestants led to an eager acceptance of such secular disciplines as education, anthropology, and psychology. Ultimately, from the authors' perspective, this acceptance led to a variety of problems. For example, infatuated with schooling, the mainline Protestant churches emphasized the Sunday school as the primary agency of the church authorized to work with young children. Christian *nurture* slowly began to be equated with the best insights that could be drawn from secular understandings about schooling. Eventually children were expected to come to faith through the primary agency of the *school*, but such education has not worked.

Again we return to language and the worldview that informs it. A church actively embracing an enlightened secular understanding of the world believed that it would thereby distance itself from the excesses of a traditional theology dominated by sin and conversion. Experts would be equipped with the tools of relevant disciplines, and faith would be taught to children. But even as the mainline Protestant churches distanced themselves from Edwards and conversion, they transformed Bushnell's concept of Christian nurture into better Christian education (read: more schooling). Although this move mirrored what was occurring in American secular culture, the resulting professionalization, secular adaptation, and privatization of the church led to practices that often devalued community and made little or no sense. For example, the assumption that schooling was of paramount importance often meant that age-graded church school programs met *at the same time* that adults gathered for worship. If worship is said to be the way the gathered community of faith responds to God, this practice often unfortunately removed children and youth from the one place in their lives where three generations regularly met in communal response to God.

It is easy to forget that the languages, practices, and customs of secular disciplines are, in reality, faith systems. Such systems suggest particular ways of seeing and being within the world. The school is an example. Rarely, however, have Protestants been clear as to how the informing metaphors of the congregation have been submerged within the metaphors presented by secular disciplines. The resulting myopic acceptance of the Sunday *school* as the only way to educate in the faith trivialized the multifaceted role of the congregation in the lives of young children. The authors reject any philosophy of children that positions the school as the primary place where a child's faith experience occurs. (For more about this see chapter 5.)

Although Bushnell's relational way of perceiving the process by which the young child comes to faith is, in fact, more helpful than Edwards' call to conversion, Bushnell would not fully accept this book's argument in favor of experience, transcendence, and participatory knowledge. While a partial recapturing of Bushnell's idea of Christian nurture would emphasize the relational, multifaceted process through which children come to accept and own their faith, a fuller understanding of how children come to faith may be gained by utilizing the work of Rita Nakashima Brock, a theologian whose emphasis on vulnerability offers a new conception of "original sin."

ON BEING VULNERABLE: CHILDREN IN PRESCHOOL

The idea that sin comes with birth and automatically permeates all of human existence is naive, suggests Brock, author of *Journeys by Heart: A Christology of Erotic Power*.[9] Brock knows that children who live at the limit of their being often are crushed by those obstacles (those "dragons" of chapter 2) surrounding and blocking transcendence. She understands, for example, the implication of the statistics reported by the House Select Committee on Children, Youth, and Families that children in the United States "are more likely to die before their first birthday, be killed before they reach 25 or live in poverty than children in 11 other industrialized countries."[10] Given such a statement, it is easy to recognize why Brock posits that the vulnerability associated with child abuse is central to her "theology of the heart."[11] It is because relational existence is at the very heart of our being that we are necessarily vulnerable by nature and easily damaged. Such vulnerability, states Brock, "is both the sign of our connectedness and the source of the damage that leads us to sin." She continues: "I believe understanding sin *as damage* enhances responsibility and healing instead of miring us in blame and guilt."[12]

For Brock, sinfulness is "neither a state that comes inevitably with birth nor something that permeates all human existence, but *a symptom of the unavoidably relational nature of human existence* through which we come to be damaged and damage others." Sin necessarily is a consequence of what Brock calls original grace, our radically relational nature. This radically relational nature is, in her words, "a basic unavoidable principle of existence." All brokenness is a consequence of such relational existence, and "sin is a sign of our brokenheartedness, of how damaged we are, not of how evil, willfully disobedient, or culpable we are." Therefore, for Brock,

> Sin is not something to be punished, but something to be healed. That we exist at all is a sign that the destructive relationships of our lives have not been final and that we have the responsibility of acknowledging our connectedness to others and our commitment to the creation of right relationships.[13]

Sin—a sign of our brokenheartedness—occurs because our relationships have the capacity to destroy or to heal. When we acknowledge that we were created for intimate, relational living, then we begin "to find grace to embrace and to heal the damage and suffering of our deepest selves and our society. Original grace is this healing gift, a reality that begins at birth."[14] Such healing occurs when people are open to follow their hearts. Following and finding one's heart "requires a loving presence," a person who helps us face the past squarely, "without nostalgia, without romantic heroes and heroines, and without numbness."[15] This occurs when we have "a safe and nurturing environment for remembering."[16] When caring individuals come together within a safe and nurturing environment, the resulting strong and caring relationships indicate the divine presence of God within our lives:

> As the dancing mystery of the sacred, the magic of connection is the confirmation of divine presence in human life. This power affirms, creates, and is re-created by heart. It is the very foundation of our lives and the center of an energy that compels us to search for the whole of life, which is its fullest ongoing incarnation.[17]

A church committed to such an understanding of the power of human relationality and the importance of safe and nurturing environments in the lives of young children will be about the structuring of community-based programs that embody (incarnate) these caring qualities.

One such program in the United States is the church preschool movement. We know, according to a major study of the National Council of Churches, that the local parish is the premier houser of child care in the United States.[18] We also know that while some of these preschool programs are understood to be an integral part of a particular church's mission and identity, others operate on a profit basis, and still others are often simply another way a church allocates the pragmatic use of empty weekday space.[19] The authors believe, however, that while child-care programs can be an important ministry of the church, some preschool programs can hinder religious growth when the church uses them primarily as opportunities to transmit cognitive information that children cannot understand instead of supporting children's multifaceted experience. In the range of options suggested by such programs, the language of the preschool professional *and* the language of the religious educator can be used to inform each other. When this happens the helpful environments and the teaching relationships described by Brock can be realized.

Brock is clear: children are vulnerable because of their relational existence, and children need safe and nurturing environments in which loving presences help them face the past and present squarely, without flinching. In this process, adults must take the responsibility of protecting young children. When children are caringly protected, to use the language of this book, they spiritedly transcend imposed limits and move into a future marked with hope instead of despair. When this occurs in a caring preschool, examples like Benton's, in the following section, are not unusual. Benton is a child who is "sailing out into the unknown" and who is in danger of being devoured by those personal and systemic "dragons" that lurk where people "fall off." The "human face of God," however, can and does occur within such church-housed preschool programs. This is a sign of covenant.

BENTON'S FLOODED MOMENT

During story time at a church-based preschool, Benton crawled into his teacher's lap and bit her. The entire week had been problematic for Benton. A pattern had seemed to emerge since Benton started preschool six weeks ago. The first part of the day, when the children chose their own activities, Benton could be found in the block corner building stall-like structures around the rubber zoo animals. Sometimes his animals would growl and bite at one another, but

Benton remained in control. It was during the period of teacher-directed activity that Benton exploded into a kicking, hitting, and grabbing whirlwind of behavior.[20] When he listened to a story at home he sat in a special adult's lap, turned the pages, talked about each picture, and had the adult all to himself. In the preschool things were different. There Benton was pushed beyond the limits of his known experience. A Judeo-Christian theologian might suggest that Benton was experiencing a flooded moment, for like the Old Testament figure of Noah in his ark, Benton was far from shore. Not only couldn't he see land, Benton didn't know how to row! So Benton bit his teacher.

Benton's efforts at transcending his situation emerged in biting behavior. Some children bite for other reasons, but Benton was angry and was making an impact when he bit. And when he bit, adults and children paid attention to him. Benton was communicating that all is not well. Many of us have had experiences with adults who have never moved through and beyond Benton's biting stage. Perhaps as young children some of these adults had been thrust into unknown terrain without adult support at very early ages. The unknown *successfully dealt with* can provide a solid basis for hope. The unknown *unsuccessfully dealt with*, if consistent, can provide an inadequate basis for hope.

With this thought in mind, we—as teachers, ministers, and care givers—are at a critical junction with someone like Benton. Benton, to use Brock's terminology, is *vulnerable*, and he desperately needs to sense, deep inside, that this place is a place where he can belong. Benton's behavior could be met with harshness; certainly adults might justify all manner of punitive discipline (an unfortunate use of the term). The authors' argument, in contradistinction, is to follow Brock's logic; to reconnect relationally and to provide a safe and secure environment for Benton. Given this understanding, we can report that Benton's teacher, along with his mother, worked out a relationally safe and secure strategy to give him some support during the rough time he was having at the preschool.

For several mornings his mother joined Benton during the teacher-directed time. Benton used his mother's presence; no more biting for him as he snuggled close to his mother during story time. Benton's teacher shortened the story time, intentionally beginning each period with the same finger play and ending with the same walking song. She decided to include an informal snack toward the end of the morning's first time block of children's self-selected activities, which extended the time and opportunity for the children to make choices. In addition, the snack time served as a signal to the children that this block of time would soon be ending. Later, as Benton's mother moved back into her normal home routine, Benton, with the help of his teachers, was able to negotiate each morning fairly well. In these days he seemed to move beyond his rough spot. What had been overwhelming now seemed manageable; and while he still could not identify his feelings, his interactions with others were becoming less rocky. He was beginning to participate actively in the community of his church-based preschool.

In the light of Benton's experience, the authors want to emphasize the caring, covenantal role adults can play within a safe and secure environment like a church-housed preschool. We hope to do this by introducing you to a "master teacher," Martha Snyder. For many years Snyder organized and ran a preschool program housed at Chicago Theological Seminary. From that base she embodied the caring presence Rita Nakashima Brock calls for in her work. One might ask, "How does Martha Snyder understand herself in relationship with children?"

A CARING PRESENCE IN THE LIVES OF YOUNG CHILDREN

Martha Snyder claims that children and teachers in situations like Benton's can be *Presences* (with a capital "P") to each other. Snyder suggests that to be a teaching Presence in the lives of children is to affirm, "with everything she is," that she will stand with the child.[21] She affirms the child and celebrates the child's "rich life of feeling, seeing, and intending." She does this, knowing full well that "such richness creates problems and conflicts." Nevertheless, "she is for life." Snyder puts it like this:

> A teacher is a Presence when she holds onto the vision that each child can become a full-functioning person and care for others. Such a teacher keeps saying to herself, "There is a way to reach this child. There is a little self struggling to be free, wanting to live in relationship and wanting to have fun." She keeps out of her mind labels like "problem child," "developmental deviate," "brain-damaged," and other pathological categories, and at the same time she works to free the child from present limitations.[22]

No matter what, Snyder promises, "I'm for you." She makes this claim, "No matter how hard we struggle, I will not reject you. We will always get back together."[23]

Being a caring, covenantal Presence in the lives of children implies a

> predisposition toward relation on the part of the teacher who seeks to shape the life of the student and to mediate to the student [the teacher's] life of relation with the circumambient world. Nor will the student learn effectively in the absence of a hospitable openness to that world and to those who assist [the student] in establishing satisfying relationships with it.[24]

Therefore any setting or teacher seriously concerned about transcendence and the covenant will practice dialogue of the sort that Snyder appears to do when she speaks about being present. Such dialogue "is a high skill requiring sympathetic and practical leadership based upon the will to communicate which in turn is founded on the capacity to enter sympathetically and expectantly into the minds of other persons, which capacity is evidence of transcendence."[25] Such a dialogue always views the other as a creative subject: "A curriculum of transcendence provides a context for engendering, gestating, expecting, and celebrating the moments of singular awareness and of inner illumination when each person comes into the consciousness of [his or her own] inimitable being."[26] Such a curriculum of transcendence is characterized not so much by the objective content of what is being studied "as by the atmosphere created by those who comprise the learning community."[27] The preschool can become the "sacred space" spoken of in chapter 7. Here is where "truth" gets told about "experience" within a "convenantal understanding." Here is where a teacher becomes a caring presence in ministry who invokes a kind of "sacred space" in which transformations occur on a daily basis.

When the authors taught a course titled "The Church's Teaching Ministry with Young Children" at Chicago Theological Seminary, we introduced students to Martha Snyder's dialogues with young children. Students were surprised and skeptical that an adult could communicate with children in such a person-to-person way. We explained that Snyder's form of communication with young children should not surprise us, because competent, early-childhood professionals make such person-to-person communication the norm of quality preschool discourse. Since few students had observed early-childhood master teachers at work, we linked this discussion with observations of other professional preschool teachers so that we were finally able to work through the students' skepticism about the reality of such relational dialogue. This incident affirms for us that those who work with young children need to be involved, early on, with master teachers in early-childhood education. This involvement is needed because such person-to-person communication as exemplified by Martha Snyder is perceived to be a rare thing by most seminary students.

But what about Benton? We mentioned how his teacher and his mother effected an intentional plan to help him negotiate his "flooded moment." But what happened later? As the school year continued, Benton's teacher made a point of talking with him about what was coming next and his part in it. When Benton occasionally refused to come to story time, she gave him the option of playing quietly at a nearby table. During the morning, when Benton would ask, "When's Mom coming?" his teacher would talk about what his mother might be doing, where Benton and his mother were in their respective schedules, and that Benton's mother would pick him up after playground time.

Early-childhood professionals might say that with the help of supportive, consistent, caring, and understanding adults like Snyder, children like Benton will gradually come to trust both the new setting as a safe place to be and the self as a person capable of functioning competently within it. In Judeo-Christian imagery a religious leader might suggest a dove with a green branch came in an act of ministry to Benton in his "flooded moment," and Benton was not alone; he had help in negotiating his way, even as the waters receded. Once again he stood on firm, dry land. Whether one uses language from a specific religious tradition or language from the field of early-childhood studies, Benton has a lot of spirit, to use Phenix' term, and a teacher in touch with transcendence will expect a hopeful Benton to continue learning, to be willing once again to go beyond his known world. Benton also has a good preschool and an excellent preschool teacher—someone able to work with his family in order to provide a covenantal, relational base in a safe and nurturing environment. Such things don't simply "happen"; a lot of hard, intentional work took place on the part of the larger community (which funds and provides space for the preschool), and the hiring of persons who are educated as qualified preschool teachers was an important priority of the preschool's board of directors.

WHERE THE WILD THINGS ARE

Sometimes, when the authors consider Benton, the need for a caring, covenantal presence and some hospitable space in which a curriculum of transcendence can occur reminds us of the ingredients in one of our favorite books for children. Max, the lead character in Maurice Sendak's *Where the Wild Things Are*, "made mischief of one kind and another."[28] Racing through the house, Max chased his dog, pounded big nails into his wall, and masqueraded in a wolf suit. When his mother called him a "wild thing," Max responded, "I'll eat you up!" and was sent to bed without eating anything.[29] Once in bed, Max sailed across many days and weeks into the land of wild things, huge, ugly beasts who threatened to eat *him* up.

Sendak has related how the "wild things" were drawn from memories of some rather unsavory relatives who used to visit his own boyhood home every Sunday. Martha Shirk relates his comments: "I hated them all. They were grotesque, with their huge noses, their great cascades of hair, their bad teeth. Worse, they ate our food. I didn't understand why they had to spoil our Sundays. Now that they have passed on, I can tell the story."[30] Confronted by these huge, hairy monsters, Max said, "Be still," and the wild beasts obeyed, calling Max, "the most wild thing of all."[31] As king of the wild things, Max led "the wild rumpus," in which he demonstrated his wildness, until he sent "the wild things off to bed without their supper. And Max, the king of all wild things, was lonely and wanted to be where someone loved him best of all."[32] So Max returned to his room, "where he found his supper waiting for him, *and it was still hot* [italics added]."[33]

In *Where the Wild Things Are*, Max "wanted to be where someone loved him best of all" and returned to his room "where he found his supper waiting for him, and it was still hot."[34] Instead of accepting *brokenheartedness* as a consequence of his relational experience—even when limits had been set and carried out—Max discovered a *Presence* incarnating (putting flesh on) the covenantal love that we believe permeates our lives.

Religious institutions have appropriate roles to play in the care and education of young children. Church leaders and early-childhood professionals have the responsibility for interpreting those roles to persons in decision-making positions within religious institutions. Such roles have little to do with the transmission of dogma and much to do with the intentional provision for the covenantal care, education, and support of young children who are asked by parents, the preschool, and the church to go beyond the limits of their known experiences. This active going beyond process is qualitatively more or less hopeful, more or less trusting. Trustworthy communities ground this process in positive ways. While negative experiences are always a part of any individual's claiming or rejecting a particular faith stance, early-childhood programs, housed in quality space with caring teachers and appropriately supported by religious institutions, contribute in affirming ways to a curriculum of transcendence that can help children as well as adults on their journey into finding and following their hearts within an expanding and ever changing world.

CHAPTER FOUR

REPAIRING RAINBOWS

IN COVENANTAL PARTNERSHIP WITH EARLY-
CHILDHOOD CENTERS, HOSPITALS, AND
OTHER HELPING INSTITUTIONS

In *The Snowy Day*, Ezra Jack Keats tells the story of how
Peter, a young African American child, awakens to find the
world covered with snow. Peter's excursion into the snow
is marked by his making snow tracks, knocking snow off
trees with a stick, building a snowman, and lying in the
snow to make angel wings. Coming home, Peter packed
away a snowball in his pocket, only to discover, when he
checked at bedtime, that it had melted. But no matter,
tomorrow would be another snow-filled day!

In commenting on the book, Keats has said, "The air is
cold, you touch the snow, aware of the things to which *all*
children are so open." He "wanted to convey the joy of
being a little boy alive on a certain kind of day—of *being* for
that moment."[1] The story of *The Snowy Day* affirms this
world and our presence within a good creation. The vivid-
ness of Keats's illustrations and the delightful story line
have made this children's book a classic.

The Christian might suggest that Peter, the small child of
The Snowy Day, stands under and within the protective
covenant of that One who set the first rainbow in the sky
(Gen. 9). That rainbow may not always be visible—par-

ticularly on snowy days—but it is there. We may be submerged in countless problems related to young children in the American culture, but the promise of the rainbow, the covenant made by God, is always present. The gentle curve of a multihued rainbow, delicately hung in the sky when rain and sun interpenetrate each other, calls to us from the biblical story of Genesis that all will be well. But what happens when a rainbow breaks? What happens when the gentle curve is twisted? What happens when hope is gone and the world seems bleak and empty?

Unfortunately, there are plenty of occasions when rainbows seem to mock the reality of human experience. For example, while the authors of this book have been married for more than twenty-five years, those years have not always been easy ones. Marriage is hard work, and after a particularly rough period during which our marriage covenant suffered considerable damage, we discovered a small lithograph of a damaged rainbow wrapped in a splint as if to protect the rainbow while its brokenness was healed. From the branches used as a splint, there sprang one small green leaf—a sign of hope. Entitled "Repaired Rainbow," this tiny print summed up the hopeful reality of our situation.[2] It was somehow easier when we purchased "Repaired Rainbow" to get on with repairing our marriage covenant.

A COMMON CALLING

Young children and their families frequently experience "broken rainbows"—an illness, a life-threatening condition, an accident, the loss of a friend or loved one, a change in family circumstances. To be about the repairing of such broken rainbows is an apt name for the ongoing process of ministering with young children in early-childhood programs, hospitals, and other caring institutions. Such ministering means that when a particular child is hospitalized and embarks on such a journey, he or she is experiencing transcendence and should be accompanied by trusted adults who represent the covenant (and God) along the way. The "dragons" that lie in wait for hospitalized children are cause, however, for considerable trauma. Bill remembers, as an eight-year-old, being wheeled into a preoperating room equipped with all manner of surgical tools in glass cases and being left alone among these instruments. He may have been left alone only momentarily, but in retrospect the moment seemed eternal. The fact that he was there to have his tonsils removed did little to eliminate the mental images of havoc he was certain were to be visited upon his body.

In his helpful book *Pastoral Care with Children in Crisis*, Andrew D. Lester leads the reader into an exploration of the ways ordained ministers can help children deal with death, abrupt hospitalizations, and other such life-shattering events.[3] Building from his assumptions that pastors often are uncomfortable or understand themselves as too busy to become involved with young children, Lester, nevertheless, argues that children are *members* of the church. No less than adults who are church members, children ought to be connected with and ministered to in appropriate, helpful ways. Outlining what children in crisis need from a pastor, he suggests principles and provides forms—art, play, story, and writing—for the pastoral care of children who have been hospitalized. Stressing that the pastor can be the "midwife" for a child's encounter with God, Lester concludes (with Brock and Snyder, as related in chapter 3) that the key to ministry with young children in crisis is to offer "a stable relationship characterized by acceptance, love, and care."[4] This kind of relational love is the essence of the covenant. But Lester is addressing the professional crowd—the ordained pastors and chaplains professionally representing God, covenant, and the church. What about the laity?

While affirming Lester's conviction that young children are members of the household of God and that ordained pastors have important roles to play within their lives, the authors are also aware that there are many persons who are unordained but who nevertheless also understand themselves as being involved in ministry with young children. Indeed, it is our experience that there are many persons sitting in the pews on Sunday mornings who powerfully resonate with the idea that their work in the world is, in some sense, an ongoing engagement in ministry. They also incarnate covenantal presence with the young child. Such a connection—between work and ministry—occurs when persons move beyond professional job commitment into the perception that God has called them into a *vocation* (*vocatio*, "call"). We believe that the church that effectively engages in ministry with young children will strongly support Lester's suggestions for the ordained minister and will also support, listen to, and help those unordained persons who understand themselves to be engaged in such covenantal ministry.

What follows are the stories of two such helping and unordained professionals from the world outside the church building who evidence through their work some of the understandings, or practices, that we sense as undergirding what we claim as vocation. Such practices suggest four core conditions we believe are always present when covenantal ministry with young children occurs. This chapter concludes with our reflections on ways the church can engage in helping such persons in their ministry and the necessity of forming partnerships among the helping professions and the church.

AUDREY WITZMAN'S STORY: R. J.

Audrey Witzman is employed by the Illinois State Board of Education. Previously she has been a teacher, a college professor, and also the owner and director of a quality child-care center. She advocates the necessity of programs that address the emotional and social needs of young children as well as their cognitive and physical needs. She relates the following event in her preschool (but with names changed). Her firm stance is that what occurred with R. J. ought to be *normative*; programs in any setting, when properly staffed, can do for other children what her staff did in relation to R. J., his family, the other children, their families, and the adults who worked with them.

When Mrs. Jackson answered the nursery school phone that late September morning, it was easy to hear that the mother was distraught. "Would you have any openings left for this year?" she asked the administrator. As the conversation continued, Mrs. Jackson learned the mother had been informed by the public school kindergarten teacher that her child was very young and also disruptive in the classroom. The teacher suggested that R. J. would profit by waiting another year for kindergarten and recommended Children's Center Nursery School as an alternative.

Later, when R. J. was enrolled, the administrator and the two teachers learned that his parents had been divorced when he was a baby. His mother, Mrs. Lancaster, had to work to help support three children. She had remarried two years ago, so now R. J. had two stepsisters who lived with his mother and stepdad. He visited his father, who had also remarried, and stepmother almost every weekend.

Mrs. Lancaster had talked with her sitter about R. J.'s disruptive behavior in school, and the sitter mentioned she had found him difficult. Not wanting the mother to think she couldn't handle him, she never discussed with her the extent of R. J.'s negative behavior.

R. J. was a beautiful child, clean and well dressed. His first day or two with his mother in attendance proved to be enjoyable for all. But when she no longer stayed with him, he started slamming doors and strutting around the classroom intimidating the rest of the children.

A week later, Mrs. Jackson walked into the classroom and noticed a parent visiting. At the same time she saw R. J. lifting a knee to smash the groin area of Michael, the boy with whom he was fighting. She gently but firmly separated the boys. The visiting parent was the mother of Johnny, who was so afraid of R. J. that he wouldn't come to school without her. The two teachers related how each day R. J.'s behavior was steadily becoming more negative, an unusual occurrence in this class, which had been together the preceding year.

Mrs. Jackson asked the psychologist at the Special Education Learning Facility to visit by the end of the week. She also requested that Mrs. Lancaster become the extra set of hands so needed in this learn-by-doing classroom.

After the psychologist's visit and a few visits by R. J. and his parents and stepparents to the psychologist's office, a conference was held for the nursery school staff, the mother and stepfather, the father and stepmother, and another psychologist. The conference lasted over two-and-a-half hours with all nine adults expressing concern. Reasons for R. J.'s hostility were discussed and ways suggested to help him become a more caring child. A program was set up to establish the limits and procedures that both sets of parents and the teachers would set for him at home and at school. The limits, both at school and home, were rules everyone could enforce. R. J. would receive immediate feedback (both positive and negative) concerning his behavior from the adult nearest him.

The conference helped solve several problems. Mrs. Lancaster told the teachers later that she had never had such a calm discussion with her former husband since they had divorced. Right before Thanksgiving she had told her husband she had done all she could. He had responded, "The rest is up to R. J." R. J. slowly began to play more positively in the sand area. His hostility became less apparent, and his positive behavior became almost equal to his negative outbursts. His Monday behavior, which had always been difficult, was slowly improving.

By December, R. J. was a changed boy. His maturity, compared to the other children, was finally showing, and he was beginning to be considered a leader. At story time he sat with his arm around Johnny, the two of them becoming more inseparable as the winter days continued.

The phone rang early on Wednesday, and the teacher who answered learned from R. J.'s stepfather that both R. J. and his grandfather had drowned the afternoon before while ice fishing. The teacher shared the shocking news with the other teacher and quickly reported to Mrs. Jackson. The three decided on their next move with the children.

They decided to say nothing unless Mrs. Jackson could reach all the parents before dismissal time. They did not want any child relaying this message to a parent who did not already know the facts. On the phone they suggested that parents share the newspaper pictures with their children and answer any questions the children had. The next day of nursery school the teachers told the children and let them discuss their own fears of dying. They also answered questions such as "Does he still hurt?" "Is he going to be put in the ground?" Throughout, the discussions reflected the love R. J. had recently shown the children and the love the children and staff had for R. J.

Later, the children were reintroduced to familiar teacher-substitutes so the staff could attend the funeral of R. J. and his grandfather. At the funeral the parents of the other children and the school staff provided a large spray of nineteen red roses representing each classmate.

One teacher, who had a way with words in time of crisis, reminded Mr. and Mrs. Lancaster of how much love R. J. had to give and how he had loved everyone enough to want to please himself and others with his self-control.

About a week later, the mother of Missy asked her where her new stuffed animal was that grandmother had given her for her birthday. Missy said at first she didn't know but finally admitted it was under her bed still in its box. It seemed that R. J. had often brought the exact same stuffed animal to school, and Missy knew she would die too if she played with that toy. Missy's mother carefully acknowledged Missy's concern and helped her understand that what had happened to R. J. would not happen to her just because they each owned the same toy.

A few weeks later, the children made a book of pictures for R. J.'s mother. They each drew a picture and talked about it if they wanted to. Mrs. Jensen wrote down their thoughts. The children shared how much they had liked R. J., and a few of them said they knew he was in heaven with their grandparents. The school presented a sand castle sculpture to the children's department of the local library in R. J.'s memory, and the children attended and presented their book to Mrs. Lancaster.

In retrospect, the staff at Children's Center Nursery School did nothing that the public school or a church-sponsored school could not have done to help R. J. and his disruptive behavior if the kindergarten teacher had had help. She certainly could not have taught eighteen other children and tried to handle R. J. all by herself. Two teachers plus R. J.'s mother in a classroom allowed a quality program to continue while R. J.'s behavior was being modified.

The staff at Children's Center felt they had had a part in the healing process between R. J.'s natural mother and father. If the parents had not been willing to communicate and cooperate, they would have found the tragedy of losing R. J. even more difficult. The four parents and six sisters all shared the loss and worked to sustain one another.

The staff rejoiced at the strides R. J. had made. There was a sense of closure as they recalled how he had learned to control his impulsiveness. This story of R. J.'s triumphs and tragedy reminds us that each child is as much potential as he is reality. The school and the family need to work together if the potential is to be realized. Schools often never know the impact their caring can have on a family or that the family can have on the school.[5]

CRITICAL REFLECTION: WITZMAN'S STORY

Much like Benton's teacher (chapter 3), Witzman's staff embraced R. J.'s experience. As professionals, they chose to work with R. J. and the other children, becoming involved in what the Russian theoretician L. S. Vygotsky speaks of as the learner's "zone of proximal development."[6] Vygotsky's theory suggests that persons reach points where they can be seen to be pressing against the boundaries, almost (but not quite) ready to move into the unknown. Vygotsky "defined the zone of proximal development as a higher level of performance that a child could achieve in collaboration with an adult or more capable peer."[7] This "almost, but not quite" state of affairs is a propitious occasion, a "proximal" moment, an occasion that can positively be helped when someone—an adult or a more capable peer—intentionally provides what Jerome Bruner calls "scaffolding." To provide scaffolding is to structure the environment in ways that help children who are pressing against the boundaries of their own abilities. For example, Witzman's staff provided scaffolding by developing a set of appropriate limits for R. J. in school and home that consistently would be enforced by teachers and parents. Once this scaffolding was in place, over time R. J. became, in Witzman's words, "a changed boy." His maturity emerged. He became a leader in the preschool. He and Johnny became inseparable friends. When R. J. and his grandfather died, once more Witzman's staff set out to discover an appropriate scaffolding for individual children and for the preschool community. Parents were involved. A process for sharing information and concerns was set up. As a group the children were told about R. J.'s death, and their concerns and experience of it were honored. When Missy "knew she would die, too" if she played with a toy like R. J.'s, the trusted adult (her mother) helped her move beyond her "stuck" place.

The authors claim that what was done was not only developmentally appropriate practice but can also be described—from within the Christian tradition—as the covenantal practice of Christian *ministry*. For example, Witzman's staff provided R. J. with "hospitable space." We would claim such *hospitality* as a central aspect, a first core condition, of all ministry with young children. The Dutch theologian Henri J. M. Nouwen asserts that for the Christian, hospitality "is our vocation: to convert the *hostis* into the *hospes*, the enemy into a guest and to create the free and fearless space where brotherhood and sisterhood can be formed and fully experienced."[8] Practicing hospitality meant helping R. J. to become a welcome part of the preschool community. The provision of such hospitable space extended to R. J.'s parents as they were encouraged to work with the preschool staff for their son. Hospitable space was there for the other children and their families as they were encouraged in their response to the deaths of R. J. and his grandfather. While other chapters (chapters 5, 6, and 7) shift to consider the hostility toward young children often found within the church, we here assert hospitality as a first core condition if covenantal ministry with them is to occur.

Hospitality implies *presence*, and a second core condition for ministry with young children is the appropriate presence of caring and challenging adults (see chapter 3). Such presence is grounded in a relational understanding of Christianity. We are created to be relational beings (as stated in chapter 2). God comes to us as person. Revelation (an "unveiling") occurs in Jesus of Nazareth, whom Christians claim to be the fullest and clearest expression of who God is and what God expects. Christians believe relationships matter. And in Witzman's story, adults are caring, appropriate, and strong presences in R. J.'s preschool experience. In concert with one another, these presences affected R. J.'s behavior so that his relationships improved. The intentionality of presence continued in the lives of those children even as they were touched by R. J.'s death. We would claim the practice of such presence as a second core condition for ministry with young children.

A third core condition is the recognition and affirmation

of the dynamic of *transcendence*. Chapter 2 asserts that transcendence is the underlying dynamic of the universe. As such, the chapter has a great deal to say about *spirit* and *hope*, words that lay the groundwork for all learning. It should not be surprising that the central celebration of spirit and hope is that world-transcending event known as Easter. Easter is an affirmation that God is indeed victorious over the injustices and wrongs that visit every one of us. In Witzman's story, for example, R. J. was angry. His disruptive behavior was upsetting the preschool class. His mother and father rarely communicated with each other. Yet R. J.'s story suggests that this staff operated out of a sense of hope and spirit that angry things could—even in R. J.'s case—be transcended. Indeed, R. J. gained control of his behavior and became a full and respected member of the preschool community. And when R. J. died, rather than saying, "That's the way life is; we can't do anything," this particular staff joined with the hopeful-spirit-filled dynamic of transcendence and covenantally commenced a "new" experience together.

A fourth core condition for covenantal ministry with young children is the affirmation and acceptance of the reality of their *experience*, a recognition of the importance of the contextual reality of a child's life. Such contextuality can be denied if adults follow a "canned" curriculum and avoid the scariness of a child's experience. In contrast, the Christian tradition emphasizes that the covenantal God is always present for us and has not forgotten us. The implications of covenant are considered in chapter 2, but the authors want to emphasize that adults are called, in our vocations, to *incarnate* (to "put flesh on") God's promise in the experience of our lives together. We are to practice who we are (and "whose" we are) in life together. And while the authors recognize that Witzman's staff might not be comfortable with this claim, we suggest that the way in which they approached the difficult experience of R. J. and R. J.'s death embodies ("practices") the covenant that we believe should be normative for all children. Such a deep covenantal understanding should pervade every child-adult relationship, and from such a base adults cannot deny or overlook the contextual experience that makes up a child's life. In summary, a developmental specialist could argue that Witzman's staff did an exemplary job in providing appropriate scaffolding for developmental growth. We agree, but we also affirm that covenantal ministry had occurred. Such ministry encompasses four conditions: (1) We believe Witzman's staff did not deny the *experiential context* of the children's lives. In addition, (2) they provided *hospitable space* that flexibly and creatively made room for R. J.'s experience. (3) Adults were present within that space and in that *Presence* were responsive to the needs, concerns, and behaviors of the children. (4) Witzman's staff assumed the deeper dynamic of *transcendence* as operative in their own lives as well as in R. J.'s, his parents, the other children, and their parents. These four conditions are critical components of ministry with young children.

FRAN TELLNER'S STORY: DAVID

We now turn from a preschool to a hospital setting in which a long-term relationship was initiated by a therapist specializing in children with a young dialysis patient. Again, to use the language of this book, it would appear that the covenantal rainbow is broken and in need of repair. Again, a young child sets sail onto an unmapped sea where dragons no doubt lurk. Can a patient transcend such limits? And if so, would one be able to recognize that such transcendence occurred, in part, because of the care (or "ministry") of the therapist?

Fran Tellner is a child-life therapist who became director

of the child-life program at New York Hospital. A child-
life therapist is a person who is professionally prepared to
work with young children and their families in hospital settings in relation to the social and emotional impact of the
hospitalization. A child-life program is a program established in a hospital or a health-care center to augment the
physical care provided for children and youth. From this
vantage point, Tellner describes her fourteen-year relationship with a very young dialysis patient from the moment it
began. (Again, names have been changed). Tellner, like
Witzman, makes no use of religious language in her story,
but the authors believe she clearly meets the four core conditions we have asserted as being central to understanding
and practicing covenantal ministry with young children.

I first met David when he was two years old and I
was in my fifth year of work as a child-life therapist
at New York Hospital. He was already in the playroom when I entered, perched cross-legged on the
table looking expectantly at me with his large brown
eyes. His mother sat to one side gazing at him lov-
ingly. Little did I know that day that this trio would
continue together for the next fourteen years; *he*
almost always waiting for *me* to provide something
new and different and his *mom* often present during
our session.

David had been admitted because he had rejected a
kidney from a cadaver transplanted when he was an
infant. This admission was relatively short. The
kidney was removed and David started on hemodi-
alysis. We did not meet for any extended work for
several years, but my clear recollection of him on
that occasion foreshadowed our long future work
together.

Three years later I was reintroduced to David on
the dialysis unit when child-life intervention was

requested by the nurse clinician. I often was asked to keep the pediatric patients from "tuning out," as they frequently did to alleviate the boredom, pain, and lethargy of medication and the disease. This assignment proved to be most challenging. I found the dialysis unit to be unrelievedly oppressive. This was an inpatient unit for those who needed close medical observation while being dialyzed. The patients were lined up in beds, one arm lying useless, hooked up to the machine. The blood flowed out, was cleaned, and flowed back in. Often patients could not sit up without nausea and cramps. They appeared to be heavily sedated, depressed, or in severe discomfort.

When I met David he was, when the television was turned off, bright-eyed, engaging, and very verbal, in effect daring me to entertain him. I eagerly presented him with materials appropriate for a five-year-old, which proved to be far above his performance level. He could not complete a preschool puzzle, he was unwilling or unable to understand game rules, and his drawings were very regressive. He was easily distracted and became quickly bored or frustrated by any project. He would revert to watching television, which was endlessly frustrating to me until over the years I learned to use it as one of the most powerful tools in our sessions together.

Working on the dialysis unit presented its own problems. The nursing staff was at first welcoming but sometimes became hostile and cutting as they perceived me as having all the fun. A meager space was provided for us therapists to store our materials, and on more than one occasion I found it bare, as a cleaning had taken place in my absence. I gradually included the nurses in parts of my sessions and spent time getting to know them separately. I respected their need to follow medical procedures and stayed out of their way; gradually they came to respect my place there and the work David and I were doing together. My sessions with David were at his bedside either once or twice a week and lasted about fifteen minutes to one hour. This schedule changed radically from time to time over the years. For the first several months I was at his command, bringing something new every time to counteract his boredom. I saw myself as playing with him, diverting him, as requested, from the hypnotic effects of television. But some days I gave in and we just watched television together. I felt like a failure at these times until I began to see that on those days we talked more, and that a particular rerun would set off a recollection or train of thought that was humorous, insightful, or just entertaining. David was a true media child, spending long hours at home watching television. His imagination was fired by it and instead of dulling his senses, it pushed him on to very sophisticated levels.

David's childlike drawings never changed much over the years. While he was very skilled verbally and drew quickly, talking all the while, his drawings were striking in their primitive execution of sophisticated concepts. This is mirrored in the juxtaposition of David's diminutive size (at sixteen he looks perhaps eight) and his very suave and social verbalizations. He has always relied on talk and quick rebuttal to deflect concern from skills that are lacking.

A recurring theme in conversation and in drawing was an obsession with Dracula. David was extremely knowledgeable about the Dracula legend, which superficially seemed a random interest, but from the beginning Dracula seemed to me to represent the "blood-sucking" dialysis machine. David often commented on his own pointed teeth, which he included in almost all drawings of faces.

He was also consistently preoccupied with monsters. It seemed to relieve enormous anxiety when he could verbalize these stories as much as he wanted to me. I never probed too much but listened and accepted and took seriously his concerns. He was more open and straightforward with me than with other staff and family, and he did not feel that he needed to conceal everything behind humor.

Tape recordings soon entered the picture as a permanent component of our work. The tapes began with original radio shows complete with commercials, which David recorded. He often played all the characters, as he was never happy with dialogue I made up on the spur of the moment. He sometimes assigned roles to staff members and was a master at involving the ward clerk, the nurses, and even a passing physician. At these moments there was no vestige of the passive dialysis patient, as he orchestrated a complete show and the room seemed to become a sound stage for a few magic moments. The value of these moments is incalculable, but I knew his self-esteem and confidence soared.

David also produced more serious tapes, and for the most part I was content to let him speak in his own voice. I made no pretense at doing psychotherapy with David, since that is neither my training nor my inclination. I was interested in providing him with the tools to express himself and the accepting atmosphere in which he could say what he wanted without fear of ridicule, rejection, or retraction.

David has always had a very clear sense of himself and how much to reveal, useful defenses, in other words.

These tapes represent the most intense period of our work. David was entering adolescence chronologically and biologically, but in many ways emotionally and physically he was still a little boy. I was unsure of myself and sometimes felt over my head. Fortunately I was able to tap into my network of social workers, clinical nurse specialists, and psychologists to help me "hang in" and stay with him, if only to listen to his tirades. During this time he successfully forged a new and positive relationship with his high-powered father, who had not figured much in his childhood. David and I also found a new way to be together, as our bedside visits were becoming tired and uninspired. He seemed to require a social context for our meetings, so we began to have lunch in the cafeteria on a regular basis. Following lunch we visited the playroom, where he got to know several of the child-life staff members. He enjoyed his visits there very much and began to regard us all as friends. We really comprised a very important social contact for this young adolescent who was in a special class at school, had very few friends, and spent most of his time at home with his parents.

I have only been able to highlight certain aspects of our work in this format. I would like to stress the importance of a child-life therapist in the life of a chronically ill child. I was the one stable person in David's treatment, which gave me the opportunity to witness the overwhelming numbers of people he encountered over the years. I saw him go through rough times and helped him emerge intact and move onward into his next stage.

Most recently David has been concerned with his mother's back surgery. He suggested a postoperative visit to her (she was in the same hospital) and proudly took me to her room, saying how grown up he felt. There continues to be a huge gap between his physical and emotional growth, but he does not give up, and with support, maintains a realistic sense of who he is. He enjoys his life, has expanded his activities and interests, and is planning a trip to Florida at the invitation of a dialysis nurse who moved there several years ago. He is understandably excited and anxious about the visit and says, "For a kid my age, there's an awful lot I haven't done."

So he is now ready to move, if somewhat tentatively, into the larger world, and I'm excited to be there to offer what assistance I can.[9]

CRITICAL REFLECTION: TELLNER'S STORY

Tellner also embodies, in her ongoing work with David, the four conditions central to the core of covenantal ministry with young children. (1) She is informed by the *experiential context* of David's life. David, a young child who continued throughout his adolescence as a patient, is someone who has "one arm hooked up to a machine." Tellner learns that such children "tune out" to alleviate the boredom, pain, and lethargy associated with treating this disease. She checks every possibility in her network to help her continue, all the time aware of the nausea and cramping normally associated with the mechanics of dialysis. One might argue that Tellner cannot avoid David's context, but what may be sensed from her story is that she is constantly aware of and will not turn away from the impact such treatment has on David. The authors claim that she embodies the repairing of the rainbow mentioned at the beginning of this chapter; she is the "human face" of a God who will not forget and who—covenantly—is with us in the midst of our experiences.

(2) Tellner, informed by David's experiential context, struggles with the second core condition—that of providing *hospitable space*. At first, she was almost overwhelmed by the experiential context of David's life as a dialysis patient. Once she accepted the context, however, she embarked on a never ending struggle with television, plays, tapes, drawings, and conversations. This was *never* easy, and one can overhear the concern and conflict all along the way. Hospitality, in a deep sense, suggests that we care enough to argue, to touch real feelings, to share—in the risky space open between us—things that deeply matter. Tellner conveys her struggle to provide such hospitality. Often she confesses her failure. And yet—even during David's adolescence—she is able to introduce a social time for David by simply sharing a meal with him in the cafeteria. She provides, once again, hospitable space.

(3) The third core condition for ministry with young children is that of *presence*—a relationship that affirms and that remains (appropriately) on David's side. Tellner can describe this relationship: "One is sick and one is well; one is a child and one is an adult. These two have become good friends over the years. As in all friendships, there have been good times and bad times—with laughter and tears, closeness and separateness." The relationship is not one-sided; she emphasizes the importance of her relationship with David for her own growth:

> I think it is not only possible but necessary for each of us to have a long-term relationship in our professional lives. It helps to keep us grounded.... For me, David provided continuity in a setting of continual admissions and discharges. I was able to return to him again and again through my years as a

child-life therapist and eventual promotion to child-life director. He kept me in touch with the world of children when I became overwhelmed with management and the bureaucracy. We evolved together along our separate paths and became friends in the process, both of us giving and receiving an enormous amount.[10]

Tellner's story offers us, in Lester's words quoted earlier, "a stable relationship characterized by acceptance, love, and care."[11]

(4) And it was always assumed by Tellner that, despite David's agony and her ongoing struggle, David would (with *spirit*) *transcend* many of the conditions imposed upon him by his illness and leave his mark upon the world. This is, of course, the fourth core condition, that ministry within the Christian tradition assumes that Easter is a reality and not just a ceremonial celebration. Tellner concludes her hope-filled story with David's words: "For a kid my age, there's an awful lot I haven't done."

Again, while neither Tellner nor Witzman would suggest that what they do is the practice of covenantal ministry, it is clear that their professional vocations have drawn them into the lives of young children, lives that are consistently "on the edge" of their very being.

ADVOCATING A PARTNERSHIP

A major responsibility of a church in this area, the authors believe, is to gather such persons together in order appropriately to name, nurture, reflect, and empower (out of the rich resources of the church) their vocations. Wherever adults meet young children on an ongoing basis, the church has powerful resources that can be used to strengthen their vocation with young children. That this is a potential partnership should not be denied; the church is called to practice its theology in conversation and partnership with those who work with young children. A simple suggestion toward such partnerships might be for a pastor to host several conversations with a cluster of intentionally invited persons who work with young children *in order to listen to what such work entails.* Listening could lead to a further exploration of advocacy—an insistence, for example, that early-childhood professionals should be properly prepared and adequately compensated. Through such advocacy the church could work for local, state, national, and global policies promoting the welfare of young children and their families.

Lisbeth and Daniel Schorr, in *Within Our Reach: Breaking the Cycle of Disadvantages,* point out that we now know how to deal with the things that get in the way of children growing into adults who can adequately care for themselves and their families. What often is lacking, they suggest, is *the will to do* what we know can be done.[12] For example, R. J. and David came from families that, despite their problems, knew how to find and provide what their children needed. In this respect, both David and R. J. were privileged. But what about those children whose families do not have such resources and do not know how to find them? What if such resources are not available? While we know what to do, we don't know how to bring together agencies (including the church) into a covenantal partnership focusing shared concern for the welfare of all children.

What we might learn from examples like Audrey Witzman's and Fran Tellner's is that working in isolation with children inside the church is not the only place (or even the best place) where ministry with young children occurs. Churches must become active players within the total culture affecting children's lives. Paul Tillich phrased this concern in a helpful way when he wrote, in *Theology of Culture:*

"We can speak to people only if we participate in their concerns; not by condescension, but by sharing in it."[13] Partnerships dedicated to unraveling the intertwined issues facing young children develop from conversations with persons like Fran Tellner and Audrey Witzman. Such partnerships require time, resources, commitment, communication, and creative thinking on the part of hospitals, churches, schools, families, and communities. The authors agree with the Schorrs, however, that caring adults know how to deal with those things that restrict the care and education of our youngest children. It is essential that we ourselves *spiritedly* enter the arenas where decisions affecting children are made, affirming that we are advocates who are concerned for the welfare of *all* children.

CHAPTER FIVE

PRACTICING THE PRESENCE OF GOD
EDUCATING THROUGH CONGREGATIONAL EXPERIENCE

When our daughter Michal was five years old, we took a summer vacation. One Sunday morning, arriving a little late at a strange church, we met the pastor and then followed directions to the room for Michal's age group. Stepping into that room, we could see the back of the Sunday school teacher, who was busily engaged in chewing out a small boy who had apparently wiggled and was having problems sitting still on the circular rug in front of the teacher's piano. We watched his eyes as the teacher let him know that he was, in her words, "a bad boy"—in fact, he ought to be "in the baby room!" Finished (at last) with the small boy, the teacher turned to her piano and, with a flourish, stated, "Now, let's all sing 'Yes, Jesus Loves Me.'" We backed out the door and went outside to collect pine cones from the church's front lawn. Something other than love was being taught in that particular Sunday school room.

Bill later had occasion to speak informally with the pastor of that church. Recalling our visit, the pastor had a specific response to Bill's story about the Sunday school teacher who sat at the piano. The summer Sunday school teaching positions were filled by "anyone willing to volunteer for a one-month teaching assignment"; that is, the pastor was telling Bill that the teacher who sat at the piano was "a warm body who filled a teacher slot" and who "didn't know the children" but who "meant well, and did the best that she could do" over four summer Sundays. And that "revolving-door" policy was acceptable, the church and the pastor had rationalized, because "anyone could take care of little kids."

THE TEACHER WHO WANTED TO SING ABOUT JESUS, AND HIDDEN CURRICULUM

While we cannot draw a firm conclusion from this brief observation, we can note that this pastor and the teacher did not recognize the toxicity of their church's ministry with young children. Educators caution us to be careful about what "the hidden curriculum" teaches. By this phrase is meant that the common, everyday arrangements connected with educational practices in specific contexts often carry hidden messages—about power, privilege, valued norms, and systemic structures—far more influential than textbook curricula.[1] The lesson learned on that particular, long ago Sunday had little to do with the church's named curriculum and everything to do with hidden curriculum.

Given this concept of hidden curriculum, what does the Sunday school teach? Is it possible that the overall system of the contemporary Sunday school can have a hidden curriculum every bit as destructive as the story about the teacher who wanted to sing, "Yes, Jesus Loves Me"? Before we can answer this question, we must first consider the history of the Sunday school.

Transported from Robert Raikes' charity venture in Sooty Alley, Gloucester, England, and moved across the Atlantic Ocean to the fledgling United States, the Sunday school was initially controlled by the laity, was highly evangelistic, and had no official connection with any denomination. A powerful movement, it swept this largely Protestant nation. In a few short years, however, the American Sunday school became denominationally focused, and by the close of the nineteenth century it was increasingly dependant upon borrowed expertise from both the public school and the seminary.

The year 1903 saw the founding of the Religious Education Association as seminaries rushed to graduate increasing numbers of women directors of religious education (D.R.E.'s). What had happened? Among other things, the public school movement, grounded in the separation of church and state, had swept the nation. While the public school transmitted the dominant Protestant ethos, denominational leaders nevertheless recognized the public school's essentially secular base and therefore "took over the Sunday School as a department within their organization so they would have a place to teach their beliefs and practices."[2] Commenting on this takeover, the respected Presbyterian educator and theologian C. Ellis Nelson concludes: "In a subtle way over half a century, the Sunday School became the chief agency of education in Protestant denominations because they needed a place to teach their doctrines when public schools, by reason of the constitution, became secular."[3] Thus emerged the peculiar nature of the Sunday school as the internal school of denominational congregations within which children of Protestant persuasion would be taught the faith. According to the canons of the popular culture of that day, children belonged in school. Quickly accepting the "gospel" of the school as their own, many Protestant churches made certain that children and young people were housed in Sunday "schools" at the same time adults gathered for common worship. Eventually nothing else in Protestantism—not worship, mission, fellowship, service, congregational life, or spirituality—would remain open to the presence and active participation of children.

Children—in and out of the church—belonged in *school.*

Looking back, we can recognize how the Sunday school "was a success at that time because it fitted into a social situation characterized by a Protestant ethos, a time when churches had great influence over individuals and communities, when ministers were among the best educated leaders, and home was the place where Christian character was formed."[4] This context is no longer today's context. Protestants are no longer in charge of a dominant Protestant national culture. In fact, "many of our symbols, appropriated by the adherents of what is often called our national 'civil religion,' have lost their hold on our personal and corporate imagination."[5] In addition, present-day Americans have begun to speak what some have called a new language, emerging from what Robert N. Bellah in *Habits of the Heart* has called the autonomous, middle-class embrace of corporate and therapeutic values; the language of rampant individualism.[6] We can claim that the old context of a nationally based Protestant home-church-community consensus (if it ever existed in pure form) is dead, and yet the Sunday school lives on as the primary educational agency of the church. An unfortunate consequence of this process is that the church assumes that children are to acquire faith solely through the agency of the church school, but given the new context and our understanding of hidden curriculum, what does such a school actually teach?

ACCOMMODATING THE CORPORATION AND THE SCHOOL

We know that the concept of the American corporation, developed at the same time as the Sunday school, was embraced by mainline denominations. This occurred at about the same time denominational officials were taking over the Sunday school. The eventual result of this merger of corporation and school was what some have come to call "the clergy pyramid." Mirroring corporate culture and caught up in the competitive individualism of America, the "top" of that pyramid was reserved for the "senior" pastor of the large church, a person who increasingly came to model himself (intentional gender usage) after the administrative practices of late nineteenth- and early twentieth-century chief executive officers (CEO's). Central to the efficient management of a particular congregation's clergy pyramid was the invention of "departments," middle-management levels of ministry over which senior pastors exercised administrative authority. The Sunday school became one such department. The Sunday school director became, in effect, the middle manager of a department within the church corporation. Allen J. Moore uncovers certain aspects of this hidden curriculum when he suggests that "the 'schooling' model of education that has generally been adopted by public and religious institutions is formulated largely around managerial and industrial concepts." Moore notes, "Not only does such an education model assume large financial investments, but it also requires heavy use of material resources, technological tools, and bureaucratic structures." In this fashion, education (whether it is public education or Sunday church school education) becomes "another form of production in which the end product is determined by behavioral objectives and in which control is central to the learning process."[7]

Ministers who accepted responsibility for the Sunday school were understood to be entering the lowest rung of the clergy pyramid. "Real" ministers left these entry-level positions as quickly as possible and advanced "up" the clergy pyramid. Those who were left behind were always regarded as either failures or odd ducks. Older ministers and denominational leaders rarely stated it that way; instead, they talked of the "seasoning process" needed for young ministers. There was one exception to this procedure. Lifelong positions in religious education were equated with "women's work"; those unordained women (the majority of graduating women seminarians through the 1970s) who survived seminary would become D.R.E.'s or M.R.E.'s (directors or masters of religious education) within local congregations. They would administer the Sunday school.

In the seminary where Bill currently teaches, many women have uncovered this hidden curriculum, become conscious of their traditional position on the clergy pyramid's lowest step, and refused to identify themselves as religious educators. Other issues are certainly involved, but many women who seek positions of ministry within the church have come to understand and resist the subtle implications of becoming directors of religious education within the clergy pyramid. More to the point, the Sunday school as a form best suited to the values and assumptions of an individualistic, mechanistic, male-oriented, corporate culture fails on most accounts to provide the hospitable space in which, using Craig Dykstra's words, the church can faithfully attempt "to *understand its own experience.*"[8] In effect, the hidden curriculum of the corporation-Sunday school promotes a set of values ultimately toxic to the church and its children.

UNDERSTANDING THE CHURCH'S EXPERIENCE

Despite this failure, most congregations continue to struggle with the needs of the Sunday school, actively repressing conversations that broach the "big" question: "Why Sunday *school?*" Dykstra is suspicious (and rightfully so) of any church that avoids critically reflecting upon its own *experience.* V. Bailey Gillespie suggests that *experience* means, in the Latin present participle, "to prove," "to try," or "to test." "Putting something to the test" thus suggests wanting to "try out," or *experience*, the particulars of an idea in real life. *Experience* therefore carries a "passing through the waters" kind of meaning; "experience is what happens to you when you actually live through or undergo an event. *It is what happens to you.*"[9] Gillespie suggests that the difference between generic experience and an experience that takes on religious significance "does not so much have to do with the types of events and information experienced, but rather the way in which these events and the actual occurrences are interpreted and felt by the believer. One attaches religious meaning to all kinds of experiences."[10]

Gillespie continues: "We cannot compartmentalize religious experience by treating it as a special area separated from the rest of living."[11] He makes this claim: "The presence of God, if it is real and everywhere in this world, is always accessible, present, and transcends all of living."[12] In other words, the Sunday school is only one place where children can reflect upon the religious significance of a particular experience. Given this argument, it is easy to see how the church could actively structure and claim a variety of experiences as educational—school, service, worship, prayer, fellowship, and pilgrimage. The forms such experience could take are endless, but they are not neutral; they are central to the educative process and an organic part of the identity of a particular congregational vision. We might say that such forms indicate where the heart of a congregation lies; this is what we, as a congregation, believe *and practice*.

When considering the structure through which the religious education of a young child occurs, C. Ellis Nelson argues that "the issue is the *form that is supported in a community where a person is nurtured*. If that form is one in which faith in God is absent or ridiculed, children will develop that predisposition and make it their own unless challenged by ideas or events of a different sort [italics added]."[13] Congregations "educate" both children and adults by "practicing" the experience of community, of worship, of prayer, or of service. Given any or all of these practices, the religious educator is called upon to help a particular congregation understand its own experience (where its "heart" lies), and then to *nurture* and to *challenge* the forms such experience takes.[14]

There are congregations, for example, that understand themselves as called and experientially connected to concerns of *justice*. In one such congregation known to the authors, several years ago a number of adults gathered around the Sunday morning coffeepot to discuss some thoughts stimulated by a movie, the newspaper, and the morning sermon. The movie, *El Norte*, portrayed the life and death of political refugees moving across the Mexican-United States border "to the north" (*El Norte*) and the hoped-for haven of capitalist culture. The newspaper had run a series of articles on Archbishop Oscar Romero, the Roman Catholic bishop who had been machine-gunned to death while officiating at a mass in El Salvador. The sermon was a rather straightforward biblical analysis of hospitality in the Old and New Testaments.

As that conversation developed, the minister recognized the "seeds" of a ministry. Nurturing those seeds, he challenged the coffee drinkers to a luncheon meeting on the following Saturday. From that small gathering, a task force emerged; from the task force, a year-long exploration of hospitality in an adult Bible study class. That exploration led to a proposal that the church become part of the Sanctuary Movement, which led to a series of exceptionally well attended congregational meetings. From those meetings came a congregational statement on hospitality and sanctuary, which led to the refurbishing of several church rooms to serve as an apartment for the first sanctuary family to be hosted by the congregation. These, then, became the places where religious education in the congregation occurred. Sanctuary became the educational form of this congregation. Children were involved in family conversations, were present for some of the vote-taking process, helped decorate and equip the apartment, met the adults and children who moved into that apartment, and sang songs led by the sanctuary family in worship.

The authors claim that such practice, sparked by a conversation around a coffeepot, provides the formative, ongoing, experiential curriculum of this particular congregation. But to package the form and content of this particular congregation's experience and ask that package to then serve as a template for all other congregations would, of course, amount to blasphemy. God does not work (we believe) in that fashion. Understanding the educational forms of a congregation and its people who are trying to be faithful is a vastly different enterprise, as Nelson recognizes, from the skewed notion that a school, no matter how well-equipped, "can 'teach' faith."[15]

THE FABRIC OF OUR LIVES

Dwayne Huebner, professor of Christian education at Yale University Divinity School, suggests that our preoccupation in the United States with pyramid climbing and competitive individualism is but an illusion, "an illusion converted into a way of life by our economic and cultural systems." He claims this is because our "habits of language, economy, and culture" are focused upon "individual faith, and the growth of that faith," rather than upon the ongoing "relational weaving" of the more communally oriented "fabric of life" that is central to the cosmos. In making his point, he emphasizes the ongoing reality of God's covenant with us: "We dwell in this realm with others. We do not speak of ourselves as a person of God; rather we acknowledge that we are a people of God." And then Huebner gives us the gift of these words: "We are our relationships. Our so-called personalities and habits of language and thinking are the fabric of yesterday—the way we are in relationship with the people of our past." We take this "fabric of yesterday" and weave it into "the fabric of tomorrow."[16] Regardless of our age and in whatever context we discover ourselves, we *weave* an acceptable fabric for living. This is our natural vocation. And the weavings from our past are joined with the weavings of our present, even as we adjust our looms for the future.

The authors are reminded that a conversation with Joan and Erik Erikson, "On Generativity and Identity," published in the *Harvard Educational Review*, included a set of full-color pictures of the weavings of the life cycle as done by Joan Erikson.[17] In these weavings she used a variety of rich-hued threads to represent the vital strengths discovered throughout the life cycle. Including gray threads as representative of the more negative elements of living, she noted: "No matter how much [gray] you might have to weave in, it is wonderful to see the continuity of the colors; they are fundamental, they are given, they are absolutely the roots of you—your legacy—and can be reestablished, can be nourished and vitalized in some way all through the life cycle." Erikson's weavings are like snapshots of specific moments in a person's life. She suggests that "you would have to weave in the gray to the extent that it might be appropriate in a given life history."[18] Such a process of "weaving" a life—whether figurative or literal—cannot be carried on in unitary isolation. The colors, whether gray or vibrant, represent those memories that include every person ever connected to the weaver.

For example, when our son, Jason, was three years old, we visited his grandparents at their cottage in Pennsylvania, as we did every summer. This cottage was one of thirty that comprised a Methodist Campground Association modeled after the Chautauqua movement of the last century. We were to be present for their annual Campground Auction, a communal event in which each cottage contributed items to be auctioned for the benefit of campground projects. While Jason wasn't quite certain what "auction" meant, he watched with anticipation as numerous objects were carried or carted to the community hall. At his grandmother's request, he, along with his sisters, carried several small bundles to the hall to be placed on long tables with the other treasures. During this process, Jason identified a small brown clock as something he liked.

And so we gathered for the auction. On the one hand, it was purely a social occasion during which objects were traded from cottage to cottage and some money was donated for this year's campground project; but, on the other hand, some of the objects were important antiques, and the bidding could be serious business. As Jason's parents and as visitors we weren't certain of what to expect of Jason, who had waited patiently for what must have seemed to him an endless time before "his" brown clock was chosen by the auctioneer for sale. "What am I bid for this small brown clock?" the auctioneer asked. Several offers were made, but then Jason stood and in a clear voice stated, "I would like that," his hands filled with coins. And the grammas, the grampas, and the other family members made room for this small boy with the handful of coins, and he, with the help of his uncle Norm, successfully bid for and acquired "his" small brown clock.

Looking back, we, his parents, are aware of the "weaving" that took place that day. The value of the auctioned antique clock was not as important to the members of that community as the value of the small boy in their midst. The several generations gathered in that community hall delighted in his presence, cherished his wish, and dealt with him from a stance of love and respect.

Ross Snyder once stated that the person sitting next to us "is really a whole colony of persons, of inner inhabitants, of people met all during a life." He continued: "Something of these people has entered into this person forever, so that the person sitting next to you is really a community."[19] Our son, Jason, carries deep within him affirming moments such as this auction, when a cross-generational community "wove" him into their fabric, and by so doing wove themselves into his life—forever. Joan Erikson, Dwayne Huebner, Jason, and Ross Snyder jointly remind us that as we are presented with the persons and the experiences of living, we weave ongoing fabrics of intimacy and community.

Our initial experience of intimacy is with our family of origin—those who knew, cared for, and helped us as we grew. Huebner—in the face of an overwhelming and often inappropriate present-day concern for the individual— speaks of the necessity of "reinforcing family fabrics" and reweaving the rips and tearings that occur and that often block the possibility of family intimacy. He also notes that it is a natural part of life's weaving for us to grow and to establish new relationships of intimacy outside our family of origin. Through such relational commitments outside the family, he suggests, persons "eventually reach the most transforming depths of human love and sexuality wherein new being is again created."[20] But this being is meant for community, not self-sufficient, individualistic isolation.

While communal fabrics lack the rich depth of family intimacy, children who are experiencing intimacy with adults in family settings are nevertheless "partially woven" into the extended, communal, adult worlds of work, of recreation, and of worship. While these activities rarely overlap in most American contexts, Huebner suggests that the educational task of the worshiping community is to help people to find God's presence or absence in their communities of re-creation and of work and in their relationships of intimacy. The "religious tradition," according to him, helps us imagine "how we can practice the presence of God in these relationships of intimacy and community. From that act of imagination, informed by the resources of our religious traditions, we need to transform our present relationships to include God's presence."[21]

For example, it is not too difficult for Jason's parents to reflect on how God's love was present in a real and actual way during that moment when a cross-generational community made room for him, affirmed him, and loved him. They did not love him as we, Jason's parents (and his grandparents, aunts, and uncles) love him, but they loved him as a covenantal community of "adoptive" grammas and grampas, aunts, uncles, and cousins might love him. And, in Huebner's sense, Jason's experience partially wove him into our adult world. Today we, his parents, can step back from that past weaving, and we can affirm, "Yes, something positive took shape that day. We can tell this story. It suggests hope rather than hatred; love rather than greed."

PRACTICING THE PRESENCE OF GOD

When Huebner wrote his article on finding God in the relational experience of intimacy and community, he curiously entitled it "Religious Education: Practicing the Presence of God." Reflecting Brother Lawrence's belief that such practice should occur continuously and that such practice weaves or connects memory and imagination within personal and communal experience, Huebner specifically rejects the idea that religious education can "become a place, such as Sunday School; or an activity with others, such as teaching; or special materials, such as a curriculum or study materials." Instead, "religious education can be a way of "integrating the personal and collective past into our lives, such that the new life that we are revitalizes and transforms the collective past."[22]

When a person or a community of faith engages in such education, it begins to "image the future, and to make some effort to shape that future in terms of how we value the personal and collective past." Huebner concludes: "The expression, 'religious education,' then, is not only a pointer to places, times, techniques, materials, organizations or activities. It is also a pointer to a way of thinking about what we do and how we are with God and others in this world."[23] The authors take Huebner's words to mean that Protestants have often split religious education from the experience of living; and, to the degree that we run schools that do not intentionally connect the resources of our tradition with the relational, experiential "weavings" of our lives, we have not engaged in true "religious" education. And we would agree.

Religious educators, therefore, are making a critical mistake when they gallop, like the Lone Ranger, rough shod into the relational "story" of a congregation and proceed to unload their saddlebag of "silver bullets" (the latest curriculum, the current administrative solutions, the best teaching methodologies) without listening for the secrets, the pains, the joys, and the troublesome worries that are packed into the communal experience of the congregation.

The authors applaud the tactic of one religious educator who stated that during his initial year in this new (for him) congregation he would maintain what was in place while setting out personally to encounter and listen to every person's version of the congregational story. Much later he reflected on how he could only describe that first year as an extended mating dance of the whooping crane, an oft-times clumsy affair marked by many false starts and exaggerated gestures on both sides as a kind of marriage took place. He said, "I was, in the jargon of anthropology, a 'welcome stranger,' I was invited to the dance, but didn't know the steps."[24]

By and large, congregations continue, even as pastors and religious educators come and go. In that sense, religious educators are always "welcome strangers." But, in order to "practice the presence of God," the religious educator must listen to, care for, and come to *know* the congregation. In Denham Grierson's words: "The task of education, when addressed to the total expression of the congregation's life, is one of calling forth, even calling out, that which is known in the depth of the people's life. In that way, through shared conversation, the collective wisdom of the community can be affirmed and celebrated."[25]

But the religious educator, even in the "calling out of that which is known in the depth of people's life" is also charged to challenge that which emerges out of the larger tradition. This is, at best, a risky endeavor, because in the present-day, secular context one quickly discovers that "since most church programs are product-oriented or goal-aimed, children are extra to the functioning of the church."[26] Children are superfluous. As a consequence of this cultural devaluing of children, most congregations continue to shunt children into the Sunday school, a place few adults in mainline denominations attend. The authors believe the secular understandings that inform this position, that continue to affirm the Sunday school as the primary educative agency of the church, and that persist in separating children from the faithful activity of the congregation, are destructive to the religious education of the child. If, however, a church is serious about the religious education of the child, then it will make room for the child within its lived experience. But many congregations face Dykstra's dilemma: "when a congregation has absolutely no experience as a church, there is nothing, Christianly speaking, for it to understand."[27] And precious little to pass on to the child.

A PROPOSAL

That the Sunday school has resisted change is well documented. In 1964 Robert W. Lynn argued that twentieth-century Protestant educators, "heirs of nineteenth-century evangelicalism, had continued their 'romance' with the Sunday school, overestimating its ability to teach their children religion."[28] While Lynn's argument was largely ignored by local congregations, John H. Westerhoff's 1976 book, *Will Our Children Have Faith?*, was highly critical of the church's continued "myopic" support of schooling and triggered a heated controversy.[29] The immediate past editor of the socially conscious *Colloquy* magazine, Westerhoff was regarded with suspicion by many mainline congregations as somewhat of a radical presence. Confirming their concerns, he attacked the Sunday school, identified liberation theology as the "most helpful theological system for Christian Education today," and argued that the church needed to become "a counter-cultural community of social change."[30] Given the moderate to conservative stance held by most church members and the general tone of the 1970s, the result of Westerhoff's proposal was that only a few congregations attempted some changes; the majority continued to support the Sunday school's resistance to any change, and the denominational publishing houses continued to crank out age-graded, school-oriented curricula that had never been field tested in any actual setting; little, if anything, changed.

During the 1980s, however, in the face of shrinking mainline denominational membership, astute observers candidly admitted that Westerhoff was right, and that the church ought to consider writing a book entitled, *Will Our Faith Have Children?* And while the authors might argue with several points raised by Westerhoff, we can agree with his contention that *experience* is "the most significant and fundamental form of learning," and that a congregation with a clear identity educates by the variety of experiential ways it carries out the implications of that identity.[31] Westerhoff puts it like this: "Our children will have faith if we have faith and are faithful. Both we and our children will have Christian faith if we join with others in a worshipping, learning, witnessing Christian community of faith." He then concludes: "To evolve this sort of community where persons strive to be Christian together is the challenge of Christian education in the years ahead."[32]

While Westerhoff and other religious educators have continued to write about the state of the church, the Sunday school, and religious education, in 1989 C. Ellis Nelson contributed "an essay in practical theology" to the conversation entitled *How Faith Matures.*[33] Emphasizing that ours is an "age of secular individualism," he also presents a compelling argument for what he calls "experiential religion."[34] He believes the problem facing the church is "how to help people *experience* the presence of God as described in our Tradition [italics added]."[35] He believes the problem, however, has a solution: "The solution is a congregation where the leaders create an awareness of God's will for present life situations through worship, education, and service. Amid such congregational life, *an individual's faith will mature through shared experiences* [italics added]."[36] Nelson goes on to suggest how a study group, composed of pastor, church leaders, and interested church members, might go about critically considering how a particular church might set out on such a pilgrimage.[37] Thus, for Nelson, the primary agency in educating for faith becomes the *congregation* instead of the Sunday school. Many people do not want to hear these words. And yet we are called to transcend old forms, to begin a risky pilgrimage. Such a pilgrimage, to use Nelson's words, is "slow and difficult, because it requires individuals to change their life-style toward a greater harmony with the values of the faith to which the congregation is dedicated."[38]

The authors find themselves largely in agreement with both Westerhoff and Nelson. We have argued in this chapter that most Sunday schools, composed of adult-led excursions within school-equipped environments, accentuate and teach values (hierarchical, individualistic, competitive, imperialistic, experience-denying, and male-oriented) of the dominant, secular culture. We have also suggested that an alternative form of learning, community-based or collaborative, focused upon the collective experience of the community (as informed by its past story and future direction) accentuates and teaches values (holistic, experience-affirming, communal, noncompetitive, and democratic) associated with covenantal learning much like that described in chapters 2 through 4. We argue that an effective and "good" ministry with young children open to intentional "education" occurs when adults are (1) caring *presences* capable of (2) providing *hospitality* in which (3) the children's *contextual experience* is honored and in which (4) *transcendence* is expected. We will continue to name these as the core conditions for the church's ministry with young children. Again, we would emphasize in the remaining chapters of this book that education need not always occur within a school setting and that education that avoids these core conditions for ministry with children can be toxic and life denying.

After our negative experience with the Sunday school teacher who sang "Yes, Jesus Loves Me," we observed and participated later that same year with pleasure in a series of collaboratively initiated and communally led events held for both parents and children from two closely related churches which focused upon themes such as "bread," "water," and "air."[39] As we shared the experience with Michal, Melissanne, and Jason in that setting—baking bread, splashing in water, and playing with a parachute— we were aware that each event was anchored in place by the caring relationships evident in the community and expanded upon by appropriate presentation and discussion of biblical concepts and stories. While the celebrative moments were, at least for us, reminiscent of childhood camp experiences, so much the better. By the time we had gathered in a circle, shared pieces of bread, the "splash" of water, and a "puff" of air, we believed that we— collectively—had *experienced*, to use Nelson's words, "the presence of God as described in our tradition."[40] And we joyfully joined together in singing "Yes, Jesus Loves Me."

CHAPTER SIX

ON THE BAKING OF GOOD, WARM BREAD

CHILDREN IN WORSHIP

> *Children must have an equal place in the worship and the common life of the church.*
>
> —JOHN H. WESTERHOFF III,
>
> *Bringing Up Children in the Christian Faith*

Bill recently baptized the child of two friends. There is, in the baptism ceremony, a fine moment when the pastor asks the parents for the name of the child being presented for baptism. When Bill asked for the baby's name, there was that moment in which Bill lifted the baby from his father's arms, a moment during which the history of those two parents flashed before Bill's eyes. Like many of their generation, they had wrestled with whether or not they should have children. In spite of their fear, in the pastor's arms on that Sunday morning was an embodiment of this generation's hope. The lifting up of that child's name in the presence of that congregation was a bold affirmation that God's love was present with this baby. Such an act is itself born of spirit; such an act is a covenantal affirmation of God's love for our time. Such an act is also an act of ministry on the part of the child for that congregation. The present age rarely admits that children often "minister" to adults. We are on safer, more controllable terrain when we define how we, as adults, are called into ministry with children. There is, however, abundant evidence that ministry "works both ways."

FEEDING THE FIVE THOUSAND AND A VERY YOUNG BOY

All the Gospels tell how Jesus, as he was teaching, once led five thousand people so far into the wilderness that the group outdistanced their supply line. They became hungry, but in that lonely place there wasn't any food. At this point, note Jesus' action carefully. He did not make bread out of thin air. Instead, he asked the crowd to bring what food they had to him. A few loaves and fishes were found, and—surprise—everyone was filled and there were baskets of food left over.

The Gospel of John contains one piece of information not supplied by any of the other three Gospels. John tells us that a very young boy provided the initial bread for the crowd. Who provides the bread for the multitude? A boy, a young boy. Remember that this crowd had gathered around Jesus to be healed, and that this young boy was surrounded by people who, at best, had come to watch Jesus work miracles, and, at worst, by people who were very sick, spiritually and physically. We aren't sure why a young boy might be present in such a crowd, but we can imagine him there, clutching a lunch of loaves and fishes, getting hungry himself.

In a sermon entitled "So That Nothing Is Lost," David Owens wonders about this young boy: "What would be on his mind? How would you have responded to a grownup asking you for your lunch?"[1] Owens continues:

I think these would have been some of my responses: "What does he want with my food? Will I get some of it back? Will the others share what they have brought? And why should I give up my lunch? I took time to prepare one, why didn't the other people prepare properly for a long day?" The boy could have thought all those things; or, he could have said, in all innocence, "Here's my lunch, take it!" Whatever the case, the real miracle of the day was that this crowd shared their food . . . so that instead of hunger, everyone was full and there were baskets left over to be collected.[2]

Owens asks us to note, in all of this:
The boy is the one who shares his food with Jesus. Even as bread symbolizes life, so the boy becomes a symbol for the way children, our children, bring life to us, bring life, health, vitality, and above all, new possibilities to us. They are not miniature adults. They are not just in stages on the way to becoming adults. They are valuable and precious in their own right. As they are right now, they have something to offer. Even with good intentions our children and their gifts are often lost to us because we isolate and marginalize them. Whenever we do this, our lives are thereby diminished.[3]

Owens, a pastor of a congregation in Illinois, presents us with the gospel's claim on our lives. Do we "isolate and marginalize" children? To whatever extent that is true, we ourselves are thereby diminished.

What does the church believe about children? Are we romantic, even as we picture Jesus in the manger? Do we view children as "real persons," or are they unfinished expressions of our will awaiting correct instruction in order that they might become something worthy of our effort? Are children "sinners" in need of conversion, "innocents" born with a clean slate, or a crazy-quilt mixture of both good and evil, vulnerable to relationships and yet capable of immense joy?

THE DISCOVERY OF CHILDREN

What do we believe about children? Recent work suggests that throughout the ages children were treated as adults.[4] This conception of childhood held through the early days of this republic, resulting in children sharing many of the same experiences as adults. By age six or seven, girls would knit, sew, weave, spin, and cook; by the same age boys (and sometimes girls, too) were hard at work on the farm.[5] Slave children regularly began work in the fields between the ages of seven and ten.[6] As small adults, children were expected to live, to suffer, and to believe in the same way as adults.[7]

The "age of enlightenment" discovered children. The theories of John Locke in seventeenth-century England and Jean Jacques Rousseau in eighteenth-century France reached the American colonies. Locke propounded that children's "slates" were clean at birth, awaiting proper guidance. Rousseau suggested that children were not evil at birth but were born in innocence. Gradually, children began to be viewed not so much as adults but as a separate and new category.

The nineteenth century expanded on the differences between children and adults. While urbanization provided ready employment for children at an early age, factory life separated children from adults and from one another. The "common school" of Horace Mann and others capitalized on the need to "Americanize" immigrant children; the result was to institutionalize the separation of children from parents via public education.[8] At the same time, the professionalization of the helping professions meant the invention of pediatricians, psychologists, social workers, group therapists, and psychiatrists.[9] Increased efficiency in birth control began to space out births and more clearly define generational differences. By 1938, reacting to data gathered by President William Howard Taft's Children's Bureau, the government voted to pass the Fair Labor Standards Act, eliminating much of the child abuse associated with paid children's work.

These historical movements, as well as others, have resulted in a mixed blessing for children. On the one hand, some children are far better off today than at any time in the history of the world. On the other hand, children are now understood to be in a separate stage of life and are viewed as incomplete beings needing to be shaped into adults. John Westerhoff, in commenting on this process, notes: "It is as if when we became aware of children and ceased to treat them as little adults, we also stopped treating them as full human beings. Now they are *only* children. It was a questionable gain."[10] He continues: "Typically, we explain that children do not know enough and cannot think well enough, feel deeply enough, or act maturely enough to be treated equally with adults. Children, it appears, have little to contribute until they reach adulthood."[11] According to Westerhoff, the discovery of childhood, at least from the perspective of the church, "has produced a serious problem; children are not valued for what they *are*, but only for what they can *become*."[12]

THE MINISTRY OF A CHILD

In spite of this history in the Christian tradition, everyone is a minister. It makes no difference if we are male or female, young or old, rich or poor, well educated or illiterate. Everyone is needed for this ministry, including young children. Have no illusions about ministry *with* young children. As adults we have more experience; thus we often minister *to* children. But children also minister *to* adults.

Consider the birth of Jesus, the Christ-child, God incarnate, Emmanuel, God-with-us, God born into this world. Surely God had many forms to choose from in becoming present among us. Yet our tradition teaches us that God became a child. The incarnation became God's definitive act of taking a preferential option for the child. The child—

dependent upon relationship, powerless, unenculturated, full of spirit, poised for transcendence—the child is God's image (*imago Dei*). Yvonne White Morey suggests, "Child is a relational term. Adult is not. Adult is a condition of law, measured from the external (from the outside). Child is internal (from the inside) and is a condition of grace." She notes:

> The measure of an adult's worth is by material acquisition or position (car, home, employment, money, knowledge, children). Yet the measure of a child is by disposition (friendliness, openness, playfulness, faithfulness, lovingness, humbleness, willingness). The contrast is as stark as comparing the words "artificial" and "authentic."[13]

After considering this contrast, White Morey comments: "How odd it is that while so much Biblical language and imagery centers on Child, so little theology takes seriously the nature of Child. Even discussions of the Incarnation focus on God's humanness and not God's childness." She concludes:

> Perhaps as the African parable suggests, until the lions write their own endings to the story, they will always be killed by the hunters. Likewise, until children, or those in touch with their childness, claim a spot in the theological *spielraum* ("playing room"), theology will always be done by "adults" from the top down.[14]

White Morey is right when she indicates the powerlessness of children within American culture and within the church; it is as if God—in that moment of incarnation—chose to enter the human condition at the lowest possible level—as a child, without economic independence, political clout, or social influence. Nevertheless, all of us (including this powerless child) are called to be God's hands, feet, arms, legs, minds, and voices; to be *bread* for those who need us—to incarnate God's love in earthy, human, caring forms. Incarnation means to give physical shape and weight to certain concepts and ideas—to be about the baking of good warm bread. When such a loaf of bread has been baked, we who are Christian know that God is present. Taste, smell, feel the bread; know that it is in the common stuff of life (like shared bread) that God is present for us.

When we are in ministry *with* (not *to*) children, we intentionally involve ourselves in incarnational, "bread-baking," interactive relationships. We will be bread for children; and, on occasion, children will be bread for us. Sometimes the ongoing process of "baking" such bread is done individually; sometimes it occurs within the worshipful response of the collective community. But whenever such care-filled "baking" occurs, we understand God to be incarnated again and again in the midst of life.

THE REALITY OF THE CHURCH EXPERIENCE

Unfortunately, when we transpose this metaphor of "good, warm bread" to the church experience of most "mainline" children, all the imagery falls flat. For example, Donald Ratcliff assesses the chances of a preschooler surviving the common worship experience of most congregations with these words: "Adult worship generally presents unrealistic challenges for preschoolers."[15] Clearly Ratcliff is correct when he summarizes the factors blocking a preschooler's involvement in the typical middle-class, American worship experience: (1) high verbal focus, (2) adult-level content, (3) resultant boredom.[16] All this, Ratcliff suggests, "translates into squirming, whispering preschoolers, which is at best distracting to adults."[17]

Ratcliff goes on to posit five alternative options for

resolving the problem of "whispering preschoolers" in common worship. The first option, his favorite, is "totally [to] separate parents and children by having developmentally appropriate content for each."[18]

The second option, his least favorite, is "meeting together for every service for the entire length of the service." Ratcliff holds that such containment "will be associated with boredom, confinement, and punishment [resulting in later adolescent] rejection and avoidance of God and church." Staying with the second option, Ratcliff suggests that "if church members are willing to change the service to fit the cognitive abilities of children, the content will necessarily need to be simplified to the point that adults will receive little." With this move, he argues, "Boredom [will be] translated into avoidance for adults as well as children." He underscores this point: "It is most difficult to challenge both adults and small children simultaneously."[19]

Ratcliff's third option is to split the morning worship with the first half leading to a children's sermon, which "sometimes works out quite well, particularly if the pastor or priest has had course work in child development."[20] He points out, however, that "the cognitive content of the music" contains "words outside of children's vocabularies."[21] Thus children will "participate in singing words they cannot at present understand."[22] And such singing, for Ratcliff, is not helpful.

His fourth option is gathering all adults and children for a brief—"perhaps ten or fifteen minutes"—opening containing "cognitively simpler songs . . . and perhaps a children's sermon." Children then would be excused to attend their own service (which might include training the child eventually to participate in adult worship). And "adults could then sing adult-level hymns and hear an adult sermon." Ratcliff concludes: "If the adults in church can tolerate some noise and disruption for a brief period of the service, this is a live option."[23]

A fifth option—that of "relying upon the church service for intergenerational ministry" is dismissed, suggesting that "family-based religious education is a far better alternative." Overall, Ratcliff states: "If children are curious or an occasional circumstance requires it, children can tolerate some of the ambiguity of adult worship."[24]

As Ratcliff's options suggest, common worship becomes the place where the theology of a congregation is incarnated regarding the place of children in the life of the church. How much room is there in this "inn"? Ten minutes? Half an hour? Ratcliff's solution is clear—two separate, "developmentally appropriate" worship services, one for children and a separate one for adults, make sense for Ratcliff, because worship is where one goes to hear God's *word*, and God's word only comes at an adult level of understanding. Worship is sermon-driven; God's *word* arrives in sermon form, carefully controlled and packaged for adult consumption. This initial assumption is linked to a second: cognitive development indicates age-graded levels of understanding. Such levels, when consistently applied to sermons, clearly suggest that children won't *comprehend* what takes place in a twenty-minute sermon. They will "squirm," "whisper," and be unable to "tolerate" adult conceptions of worship. And it is adults, after all, who dominate worship practice.

CHILDREN IN WORSHIP

An alternative stance suggests that worship is where the people of faith *collectively* make their response to God. Given this assumption, worship becomes the place where children not only make their own response to God but also experience the response of their trusted care givers, who are, after all, the "ritual elders" of the congregation. The authors grant that there are occasions when the ritual elders of a congregation will experience worship by themselves, but at base, "common worship" is where the entire *oikos*, literally translated as the "household of God," gathers in response to God. Elizabeth McMahon Jeep challenges the household of God in these words: "Taking children seriously goes hand-in-hand with taking ourselves seriously."[25] Ratcliff has made a correct assessment of the current practice of most mainline congregations in this country, but the authors believe that he has not, to use Jeep's words, "taken children seriously." We believe he has not adequately considered the theological consequences of his position or the hidden curriculum he espouses.

Ratcliff argues that certain *cognitive* levels must be reached in order to participate meaningfully in worship. By centering on cognitive development, he seems to exclude all other developmental areas. We suspect that this exclusion not only impoverishes the liturgy, it is also developmentally inappropriate. For example, should children be excluded from worship, would a congregation ever *dance* on a Palm Sunday? And if a child wants to express thanks—with childlike exuberance—that Gramma is home from the hospital, must she do so in her age-graded worship center, far removed from the place "where Gramma always sits on Sunday." And if toddlers in a Zimbabwean service of worship wander up to where mothers sit in the choir, isn't that part of being in *oikos*, the household of God? Can't we be more intentional in the baking of good, warm bread *together*?

Donald and Patricia Griggs have, for many years, directed the Griggs Educational Service, written books, and led countless workshops for the church.[26] When a new church began meeting near their home in California, they volunteered to work with the congregation. Central to Shepherd of the Hills Presbyterian Church was the conviction that children should be full participants in worship.[27] It was also assumed by the pastor and other leaders of the developing congregation that the best worship service for a child to attend is one that is the best for an adult to attend. This collective understanding—that worship can be hospitable for children as well as for adults—has resulted in a collection of stories by the Griggses as they recall in Patricia's words what happened to the children and adults in this new congregation:

On Maundy Thursday, Nicholas was the only child who joined with twenty-five other worshipers to celebrate the sacrament of the Lord's Supper. Nicholas, four years old, could have stayed home with his father, who was caring for baby brother Tyler. However, when he saw his mother getting dressed to leave for the service Nicholas asked where she was going. "To church," Rhonda said. "I want to go," replied Nicholas. Rhonda responded, "I don't think you will enjoy the service tonight. There probably won't be any other children there. Why don't you stay home and help daddy take care of Tyler." "I want to go to church with you," Nicholas insisted. Rhonda knew that he would be welcomed at the service and if he wanted to go that badly, why not.

Nicholas was welcomed. He entered the room enthusiastically. At the beginning of the service he spent time on the carpet that was near the sitting area. When the room was darkened and it was time to celebrate the sacrament, Nicholas scurried to the seat beside his mother. He was among the first six persons, with Rhonda, to be seated around the table to receive the sacrament. Mike, his high school se-

nior friend, was seated between him and the pastor.
Dr. Clark, the pastor, offered a plate of bread to
Mike with the words, "Mike, this is the body of
Christ." Mike took a piece and passed the plate
saying, "Nicholas, this is the body of Christ."
(I wondered what Nicholas would do. Shepherd of
the Hills Presbyterian Church is a newly formed
congregation and in its fifteen months of worshiping together had never before celebrated communion in this manner.) Nicholas took a piece of bread
then passed the plate and addressing his mother,
repeated Mike's words.

While the abstract meanings his mother and friend
Mike assigned to this ritual were far in the future for
Nicholas, what was present for him during the communion experience was the deep sense of belonging
within the caring community of his church.

On Easter Sunday I had the opportunity to visit
with Nicholas. We talked about the Maundy Thursday service and I asked him, "Why do you think we
were having communion?" Even though he did not
know what "Maundy Thursday" meant, without
hesitation Nicholas responded, "That was the night
Jesus had his last dinner with his friends, just before
he was killed by the soldiers." If I had had any
doubts whether it was appropriate for Nicholas to
participate in the sacrament of the Lord's Supper, I
had none now.

I also recalled the first communion service of our
little congregation, about fourteen months earlier.
Ian (age eight), Eric (six), and Nicholas (three) were
present. The worshipers were invited to stand in a
circle around the communion table. The children
immediately left their parents to stand right in front,

up against the table. They all watched and listed with fascination as Dr. Clark repeated the words of the liturgy and prepared to serve the bread and wine. The first couple of people were served; then Nicholas, tugging at his father's trouser, was lifted up and held so he could see better. He leaned closer to his dad's ear and asked in a stage whisper, "Why do we do this, daddy?" "To remind us of Jesus," replied Scott. When the elements were passed to Scott, Nicholas wanted his turn too, and was not about to be passed up.

We have been present for most of the worship services since the congregation's first. We have seen and heard many examples of ways children and adults have interacted with one another in the context of worship, fellowship, and service. On the way home each Sunday we compare notes in order to remember what happened, and then at home I record the new stories in the computer. Space does not allow us to tell all of the stories of all the children, nor even all of the stories involving Nicholas. However, Nicholas and his friends do provide a wonderful case study of how young children are nurtured at home and at church in a nontraditional setting.

There is, for example, a story about how Nicholas claimed that he belonged in worship. On that Sunday morning, we all took our seats. The children had worshiped with the adults for five weeks. They had become quite comfortable with the congregation and with the routine of worship. Where they used to go directly to the carpet area to draw, read, and do puzzles, now they usually went directly to a seat. They no longer felt that they must sit with their parents either. They often chose to sit together or with someone else. It was, therefore, no surprise when on this Sunday, Nicholas sat next to Mike, a teenager who has a wonderful relationship with all the children. Dr. Clark welcomed everyone and was about to begin the announcements when Nicholas said to him, "I always sit here. He is my friend" (pointing to Mike).

We recall another occasion when a child reached out in similar affirmation and ministry to an adult. To close worship one Sunday everyone formed a large circle. The children were scattered among the adults. Nicholas was being held in his father's arms. Eric stood with his arms around his mother's legs, and Ian was between his father and Jane Nelson. The instructions were given for each person to turn to the person on the right and say, "Jesus said go." After the words had traveled around the circle, they were to say, "Jesus said teach," then after the words traveled around the circle again, "Jesus said, I am with you always _____," saying the name of the person on the right. When everyone was clear about what each was to do, I started the words. The first words, "Jesus said go," were not repeated by any of the children. At the second set, Ian joined in. When the third set began its journey, I wondered if Ian, who was next to Jane, knew Jane's name. At that moment, when the words reached Ian, he turned to Jane, looked her straight in the eye, and said, "Jesus said, I am with you always, Jane." Tears came to Jane's eyes, as to others. The power of the blessing had been increased by the participation of a young child.

There was another time when one child reached out to another child to welcome her to the worship experience. Katrina (age two) had been coming to church with her family for a month. The first couple of Sundays she clung to her mother. To make her more comfortable and able to be near her mother without always being on her lap, I put a child-size chair next to the mother's chair at the end of the aisle next to the carpet. By sitting on the carpet and offering an occasional book to Katrina, she had helped Katrina begin to relax so the child would now sit on the carpet with me (giving her mother a break once in a while).

One Sunday another two-year-old arrived with her family. I went to get another child size chair and placed it behind Katrina's. Kendra was immediately greeted by Katrina, who took her hand and led her to the chair. She then moved her chair so it was next to Kendra's. Kendra was not so sure about all this and sat with her parents for a while. Katrina came and sat with me on the carpet to look at a book. Kendra was interested and came and sat down, too. Katrina took out her bag of Gummy Bears and ate one, then took another and stuck it in Kendra's mouth. Before I knew it, Katrina had shifted (a little at a time) until she was snuggled up to Kendra, all the while feeding her Gummy Bears. By the end of the service these two were fast friends, without speaking a word.

Several weeks after Kendra and Katrina discovered each other, Kendra came to church with her grandmother, who had never been to our church before. Kendra's parents were out of town, and grandma was caring for Kendra. "I had to bring her," said the grandmother. "She insisted she had to go to church to see her friends, especially Katrina." The trouble was, Katrina was absent this week! But, Kendra did well anyway. When they got home, Kendra wanted to call Katrina and find out why she wasn't at church. The grandmother did not make the call but told the parents when they returned, and they did call. The next Sunday both families were in church.

It has become quite obvious that the sacraments of baptism and holy communion, as well as other special services, are times the children enjoy. They participate with much enthusiasm and awe. Even though the children do not comprehend, from a cognitive perspective, all that is happening (do the adults?), they are tuned in to the affective dimensions of the services. For example, the Sunday arrived when we, as a new congregation, would have our first baptism. Dr. Clark invited the children forward during the focusing time to speak to them about the importance of baptism. He let them put their hands in the water, encouraged questions, and told them about baby Jake. Then, before sending them back to their seats, he asked them to pray with him. He reached out to take their hands while the children stood around the table with bowed heads. Nicholas, standing in the front of the table with his back to the congregation stood with arms fully extended and head bowed so low his face was almost touching the table. I could see his eyes were squeezed shut. Dr. Clark began to pray, "Dear God, we thank you for your love," pausing after the first sentence to take a breath. Before he could begin again, Nicholas repeated the words, "Dear God, we thank you for your love." Dr. Clark continued the prayer, and when he paused again Nicholas repeated his words. By this time, Dr. Clark caught on to what was happening and continued speaking in short phrases and waiting for Nicholas. The other children did not join in, which surprised us, but Nicholas did not seem to notice. When the prayer was over, the children returned to their seats, not noticing the tears in the eyes of many of the adult worshipers who were touched with the innocence and openness of a child's prayer. Later, we asked Nicholas' mother if they prayed around the table at home, holding hands, and saying a phrase at a time for Nicholas to repeat. "Yes," she said, "he did it just like we do at home."

The first Sunday of Advent had come. It was also the first anniversary of our church and, in addition, communion Sunday. We asked the children to join us around the table as we explained the advent wreath symbolism and the season of Advent. Tyler and Kendra (both two years old) were half listening and half playing under the table. While the older children were joining in conversation with us and contributing much, Tyler and Kendra discovered the bread. It was part of a larger loaf. The broken end was facing the back of the table (where the children were standing). Tyler and Kendra were about the same height as the table. Like sneaky little mice they took turns picking tiny pieces of bread from the broken spot on the loaf. When it came time for communion, they were willing to take good-size pieces of bread with confidence and big smiles on their faces.

Lauren (age ten) had asked if she could be baptized on the Sunday closest to Christmas. On December

23, she stood before the congregation and made her responses without notes or prompting—she had memorized the service. When the ritual was over, Dr. Clark asked the congregation to come forward and stand around the table and Lauren. All fifty plus of us came forward. As he does with every child, he said, "Lauren, I want you to look at every face here. These are your new sisters and brothers, aunts and uncles and grandparents. We are your family. Whenever you need us we are here to laugh and cry with you, to help you, and to comfort you. You can come to any of us any time and we will love you because you are part of this family." Then he spoke of the congregation and we prayed together.

This kind of reminder of our relationship to one another strengthens the bonds among us. It does not end there, however, for it is evident that the idea of family continues within their daily lives. Lauren, for example, went with a group from the church to hang invitations to come to church on doorknobs of houses in new neighborhoods. Part way through the day an adult overheard Lauren saying something as she put her invitation on the door. "What were you saying Lauren? That no one was there?" "No, I was just saying, 'May the peace of God be with this house.' I've been saying it every time I put an invitation on the door."

It was communion Sunday. I was fifth in line. Kendra was in line three or four people behind me. About the time I was taking the wine I heard Kendra crying her eyes out. She was obviously very upset. As I walked to the back of the room I looked to see what was going on. Mother, wisely, was leaving the line with Kendra after taking the bread. She stood with her at the back of the room watching the rest of the congregation. About four or five people were left in line when Kendra pulled her mother forward and they joined the line. This time Kendra took the bread, dipped it in the wine, and left with a happy face. After church I asked, "What was upsetting Kendra?" Her mother replied, "I was holding her, and when we got to the bread her father broke a piece off and gave it to her. She started crying and pushed his hand away. We didn't know why she was upset. But I figured out when we were standing in the back that she wanted to take her own bread and do the whole thing herself like the other children. So when we went back in line I let her."

We have noticed that the children were more than willing to contribute their part to the worshiping life of the congregation. In spontaneous as well as planned ways, there were many opportunities for children to contribute their gifts to God and to the congregation in worship. We recall several occasions when this was demonstrated. It was time for the offering. Mike and Ken came forward to receive the baskets, and then each went to a section to begin collecting the offering. Mike handed the basket to Scott and it began its way down the row. When it came to an empty seat, Nicholas, who stood up to see what was happening, took the basket and passed it to the next person in the row. When it reached the end, he took it and ran to Mike, giving the basket to him. We thought that was the end of the adventure, but it wasn't; he followed Mike and watched what he was doing. Mike, seeing that Nicholas wanted to help, began giving the basket to him and directing him where to pass it. When the offering was brought forward, there was Nicholas, standing in front of the table between Mike and Ken as the doxology was sung and the prayers were offered.

The next Sunday, when Mike and Ken got up to take up the offering, Nicholas did too. He followed Mike, who, taking the cue, gave the basket to Nicholas and directed him through the process of taking up the offering. Mike let Nicholas carry the basket to the table. We noticed during the prayer that Nicholas was holding the basket with one hand and going through the offering with the other. He pulled an envelope from the bottom of the basket and held it up to Mike, then put it back. After the service we asked Mike what was going on. Mike said, "That was my envelope. Nicholas wanted to know where I got the envelope and what was in it. So, I explained that I put my offering in the envelope and gave it to God to help the church. Nicholas told me he wants envelopes too."

The story of Nicholas wanting offering envelopes got back to Dr. Clark, who took it seriously and brought a catalog of offering envelopes to us to choose an envelope to order for the children. We took the idea to the Children's Ministry Commission, which said, "Why order special envelopes just for the children? If we are expecting children to be included with adults in worship, they should have the same envelopes as everyone else. And, if we are ordering envelopes for the children, why don't we order them for the adults too?" I told the steering committee what the Children's Ministry Commission had said. They agreed. We all should have offering envelopes. Envelopes were ordered for everyone, and the committee began talking about stewardship education for the congregation—all initiated by the spontaneous act of one small boy.

One Sunday just before the war in the Persian Gulf it was time for the prayers of the people. The children were all present. A number of joys and concerns were offered by adults, and then, Ian raised his hand. "I want us to pray for peace. My grandfather's generation had a war. My father's generation had a war. I want my generation to be the first one without any wars."

Several Sundays before the first day of Advent, Alice (age ten) came to me and said, "I was wondering, can the children do a play for Christmas for the church?" My first thought was, "Oh dear, rehearsals, time, recruiting people to help—I can't take this on." But here was a child, enthusiastic about using her gifts and those of the other children to give something to God and to the congregation. So I told her I would ask the Children's Ministry Commission The commission said, "Sure, why not, as long as it is simple and short. We don't have to be fancy." I then took the idea to the worship-planning team and they offered the responding time during the Sunday service for presenting the play. "A great idea," they said. So, I begin planning. The play had to be simple with as few characters as possible. But because a child said, "Can we?" we would have a play.

As we were rehearsing our Christmas play, Alice asked, "Why don't we have any wise men in our play?" I answered, "Because they had not arrived yet. The wise men did not find Jesus the night he was

born, but weeks or maybe even months later." "But
in storybooks the wise men are there with the shep-
herds," said Paul. "Yes, that is true. When you get
home, look in Matthew and Luke in your Bible and
read the stories about Jesus' birth. You will discover
that there are two different stories. When people
write story books or tell stories, they often put the
two Bible stories together. In a few weeks we will
have Epiphany Sunday when we will read about the
arrival of the wise men and learn their part in the
story." During this conversation several of the children (ages nine to twelve) entered in and expressed
frustration that the new Bibles for the church had
not arrived yet, so they could not read the stories
"right now!"[28]

REFLECTING ON THE PROCESS

Veteran Christian educators, the Griggses learned a lot
during the year and a half that they worshiped with and
volunteered time for this emerging congregation. Their
reflections are as follows:

> The children, their parents, Pastor Clark, and
> members of the congregation, all have been our
> teachers, especially the children. We have learned
> that children are eager to participate in worship.
> They love lighting candles, singing, praying, assist-
> ing with the offering, passing out bulletins, packing
> up after the service, and being involved with the
> adults. Behavior is seldom a problem when expecta-
> tions are clear for both parents and children, when
> there is flexibility regarding movement in and out of
> the worship area, when there are alternative spaces
> for the children, when there is the sense of being
> welcomed and included, and when there are caring
> adults whom the children know and trust.

From the beginning of this fledgling congregation there has been a clear commitment on the part of Dr. Clark, the organizing pastor, as well as the steering committee and most of the congregation, that children belong in worship. They believed the guidelines of the Presbyterian Directory for Worship, which state,

> Children bring special gifts to worship and grow in the faith through their regular inclusion and participation in the worship of the congregation. Those responsible for planning and leading the participation of children in worship should consider the children's level of understanding and ability to respond, and should avoid both excessive formality and condescension. The session should insure that regular programs of the church do not prevent children's full participation with the whole congregation in worship, in Word and Sacrament, on the Lord's Day.[29]

This affirmation is quite different from what is the common experience in many churches in our area. It has become more usual than not for a church to schedule worship and Sunday school at the same hour, though there are some churches that have two services and one or two Sunday schools. Typically, children are in worship for the first fifteen to twenty minutes and are then dismissed to their classes so that adults can get on with worship without being disturbed by the children.

One of the reasons for this normal Sunday schedule for many churches is that most people do not want to spend more than one hour, plus a little more, at church on Sunday. Another fact of life is that regular attendance for most people now is one or two Sundays a month. Long gone are the days when we were absent from church and Sunday school only when we were sick or out of town. Today Sundays are part of our leisure time and there are lots of other activities beckoning us. If families are going to give only one hour to church, then many want to be able to worship and have their children in Sunday school at the same time.

Shepherd of the Hills Presbyterian Church began without a Sunday school, placing most of its emphasis on worship. The question that was asked and responded to was, "How can we best welcome, care for, and nurture the children and their families who choose to join with us?" When a new family arrives at the door of our worship center (a multipurpose room in an elementary school) the whole family is welcomed. Everyone receives a name tag, even the youngest member of the family. The parent(s) receives a brochure that explains how children are included and cared for in our congregation. There are suggestions of how to prepare the children for worship, how to include them in the worship service, and ways to follow up after the service. Parents are directed to the child-care room and told they can take their children there at any time and collect them any time. The carpet area is explained as a place for stretching legs; it is a quiet place, not a play space. There are "quiet materials" (paper, pencils, puzzles, story books) on the carpet as well as a "carpet companion" to assist the children. The adult on the carpet calls attention to times for praying and singing and for listening to special music.

The parent(s) and child(ren) are also told about story time. This is the time during the sermon when those children who choose may leave the service with a "story companion" to hear and respond to a story related to the topic of the scripture that they heard and the sermon the pastor will be preaching. They return after the sermon to continue in worship with the whole congregation. This part of the service responds to the difficulty children and their parents have during the sermon time. It is hard for a child to listen and to understand the sermon; and twenty minutes is a long time to sit still and be quiet. Story time provides time to stretch, to move to another room, to be with a caring adult for a special time, and to be with the other children. About a dozen adults are willing and able to take turns with story time.

The major educational agenda of the church is not Sunday school. Rather, it is the Christian nurture of children, youth, and adults. There is a significant difference between these two emphases. You can have a church without a Sunday school. The Christian church as an institution existed for eighteen centuries without a Sunday school, but it did not exist without Christian nurture by parents, members, pastors, priests, teachers, and leaders. In every age it was understand that you cannot have a church without some form of corporate worship where God's word is proclaimed and interpreted, where the sacraments are celebrated, where the prayers of the people are offered, where hymns are sung, and where persons are invited to discipleship.

Shepherd of the Hills Presbyterian Church intends to develop a more structured approach to Christian education, which may include a midweek program for children and their parents, all-church retreats, special events for teaching and learning, or all of these. When the numbers warrant and there is space to conduct such a program, the leaders and members will explore ways to respond to the needs and interests of those who are involved. In the meantime, and for the long-range future, the whole congregation will worship together on Sunday mornings. And the key question will continue to be asked and responded to, "How can we best welcome, care for, and nurture the children and their families who choose to join with us?"[30]

CHILDREN BELONG IN WORSHIP

As Christians we claim that the focal point of faith is worship. In the preceding section the Griggses demonstrated how worship is of tremendous significance to both adults *and* children. Worship is where we respond to God from our lives, yet one of this book's authors, as a seminary professor, attests that he is no longer surprised to meet new seminary students who have never regularly attended church services of worship. These same seminarians are terrified about the prospect of leading something (Sunday morning worship) they rarely, if ever, have experienced. How has this state of affairs come to pass? In the 1950s we developed the one-hour Sunday experience, during which adults went to worship while the "kids" went to Sunday school. Such a split helped ease the then crowded churches, but once in place the single-hour format stuck, even when conditions changed. Once out of worship, children rarely, if ever, returned. Ratcliff's options illustrate this point. This format—with adults "off there" in one professionally administered box and children and youth "over there" in another box—effectively isolates children and youth from the gathered congregation, the household of God (*oikos*).

Is such a split, now acknowledged as a pragmatic accident of history, a good idea today? The authors of this book say no. We disagree with Ratcliff. A more theologically sound model—and one that educates at the power source of our faith—is that of the faith community gathered in worship. Here is where the people of God (of all ages, shapes, and sizes—the *laos*) come together in a space that transcends the cultural boxes and the professional roles in an open, caring, cross-age *koinonia* ("community"). Liturgy, which literally means "the people's work," is then an activity wherein a collection of lives are centered around the experience of responding to God.

The authors are not advocating "thoughts for children" in worship or the building of a "prayer corner" in a classroom; we mean common worship for all within the household of God (*oikos*). We mean understanding that, while we do not engage in worship because it is an educative act, the most powerful educative weekly moment in the parish is when we invoke God's presence ("Creator God, Be With Us Now").

There are problems with mainline denominational worship. For most of us, worship on Sunday has become a controlled ceremony, carefully choreographed. Were transformation to occur, most of us would be shocked. Perhaps our shock would say a great deal about us—nevertheless, we would argue that collectively, as a people, if we want to be about faith-shaping young children, then children need to see what parents "prize"; parents, other caring adults, and children ought to worship together.[31]

Are we advocating "kids in worship"? We are. Are we aware of the dominance of the sermon and how the addition of children would affect and even change that occasion? We are. Do we know how risky, not to mention threatening, such a suggestion would be to most C.E.O.'s (an intentional "slip," as in the pastor as Chief Executive Officer)? We believe we do know the risk. But we have a tradition that we believe grounds us; we have (historically) a vision of an intergenerational faith community—the *laos* ("laity," or people of God), united in ministry through baptism, responding to God as members of God's household (*oikos*). It is a vision of a celebrative people, filled with joy. Concerning such celebrations, Dennis Benson and Stan Stewart are on target when they note: "As every leader of worship knows, children are just as likely to interrupt at the highest and holiest moment as any other." They continue: "Perhaps this is not such a bad thing. Leaders of religious ceremonies are constantly tempted to take themselves and their liturgies too seriously." Reflecting on this arrogance, they suggest, "It was so in Jesus' day; so it is today. Could it not be that our children are sent by God to prick the balloons of our pomposity?" Benson and Stewart believe that when a congregation is willing to open themselves to children, "The current of divine life" will flow into worship.[32] They conclude:

> When this is done, worship will take on a new spirit and a new feel. It may move down the previous liturgical trail, but it will do so at a different rhythm. And all this is not the result of some upbeat liturgical design but simply the dynamic the children bring with them. Worship becomes more vital and certainly more spontaneous. It takes on a feel unlike any other human gathering. That is the point.[33]

We agree; that is the point.

CHAPTER SEVEN

BROCCOLI BEAR AND THE DISTANCE FROM EDEN
CHILDREN IN AN ABUSIVE AND OFTEN TOXIC CULTURE

Binkley, one of the young cartoon characters in "Bloom County," cautiously approaches his sleeping father to announce his completion of a "manuscript."[1] Binkley says, "I've written a children's book. It's called 'Broccoli Bear.'" Father continues to sleep. Binkley proceeds, "It's about a bear named 'Broccoli Bear' who only likes to eat asparagus. Unable to reconcile this contradiction in his life, he buys an Uzi and takes out a K-Mart." Father is wide awake and sharply attentive as Binkley concludes, "Sort of a fable for today."

In the last cartoon box, we see Binkley sitting in the midst of his scattered manuscript outside his father's room. His father has kicked him out of the bedroom and has once again prepared himself for bed and some much needed sleep. Hearing his dad loudly locking his door, Binkley exclaims, "I never said it was 'Goodnight Moon.'"[2] At least Binkley catches the tenor of our time. Hostages, machine guns, cyanide-laced products, and lost children's faces on wax milk cartons remind us how far from Eden we have traveled.

THE POWERS OF DARKNESS AND DESPAIR

Edward Hicks's famous painting *The Peaceable Kingdom* shows all the animals gathered as if for a family portrait. Animals that kill rest beside erstwhile prey, and no one gets hurt. The reality, however, is more forcefully realized in Woody Allen's send-up of Isaiah 11:6–8: "The lion and the calf shall lie down together, but the calf won't get much sleep."[3]

When Bill was eight, he got a hamster for his birthday. The hamster, however, turned out to be pregnant, a condition that Bill discovered as she was in the process of devouring her offspring. In much the same fashion, we are suddenly aware that we are eating our own children: "Child-abuse deaths up 70% in city," leaps the headline from the paper.[4] "The murders of dozens of... children went largely unnoticed by the public last year, which saw the largest number of child homicides in Chicago in a decade."[5] These were not pleasant deaths. We are talking about children who were "one year old or younger when they were shot, stabbed, beaten, strangled, or burned to death."[6] When we consider such information, and when we read that "44.2% of black children, 37.9% of Hispanic children and 14.6% of white children are living below the federal poverty level" (1989),[7] why don't we collectively rise as one person and shout, "Enough! Things must change!"?

We know, unfortunately, that the world is harsh. Young children often bear the brunt of this harshness.

- Everyday, 40,000 children under the age of 5 die in developing countries. The majority could be saved at very little cost. . . .
- The United States lags far behind most industrial nations in preventing childhood disease and injury. A quarter of preschoolers and a third of poor children under 5 are not immunized.

- Reports of child abuse in the United States have been increasing in the past decade. The majority concern cases of neglect, where children are often denied adequate medical care. . . .
- In the United States, three-fifths of the households that receive food stamps contain children. The average amount received, in constant dollars, has not changed since 1980.[8]

If we can say that Christ is the incarnation of God's love, then we must say that statistics such as these are indicators of the incarnation of evil in American society. The powers of darkness and the principalities of despair are real. Of that we have no doubt whatsoever. Today the principalities of despair have more acceptable labels, as do the powers of darkness, but they still exist. We might sanitize them, for example, by calling them "systems"—economic systems, political systems, even family systems—but systems can incarnate evil. We speak of those incarnations of child abuse, of economic deprivation, of things like drugs and babies having babies, of the logical consequences of broken community. Pain, despair, and shattered visions are real. Evil has power. Such negative incarnations are being born every day.

VOICES FROM SOLENTINAME

Paulo Freire, in *Pedagogy of the Oppressed*, argues that while animals live within limits and aren't capable of imagining anything else, humans are born with the ability to go beyond limits, to speak "true words," and "to transform the world."[9] Keep this "dynamic of transcendence" in mind and consider what Freire calls—in opposition to transcendence—the "dramatic theme of silence."[10] In situations of silence people are *not* encouraged to transcend their circumstances. Limits are imposed that surround and control such possibilities. After a while those who are oppressed begin to identify with the oppressor. Internalizing the oppressor's controls, they lapse into silence. In their identification they have accepted the oppressor's definition of reality. They have no voice.

There are moments, however, when people discover their voice. Nelle Morton documents the powerful process of "hearing into voice" someone who has been silenced:

> It was in a small group of women who had come together to tell our own stories that I first received a totally new understanding of hearing and speaking. I remember well how one woman started, hesitating and awkward, trying to put the pieces of her life together. Finally she said: "I hurt... I hurt all over." She touched herself in various places as if feeling for the hurt before she added, "but... I don't know where to begin to cry." She talked on and on. Her story took on fantastic coherence. When she reached a point of most excruciating pain no one moved. No one interrupted. Finally she finished. After a silence, she looked from one woman to another. "You heard me. You heard me all the way." Her eyes narrowed. She looked directly at each woman in turn and then said slowly, "I have a strange feeling you heard me before I started. You heard me to my own story."[11]

Morton is telling us that this is what it is like for an *individual* to be heard into voice.

Rarely, however, do we have a record of how a community, a collection of silenced souls, hears one another into voice. One such rare expression is a series of comments by persons whose experience was engaged by the Bible and whose voice became a series of vivid paintings, finally published in book form as *The Gospel in Art by the Peasants of*

Solentiname.[12] Behind the art work and the comments of the artists lies a powerful story. In 1966 a Nicaraguan priest, Ernesto Cardenal, started a small Christian commune in Solentiname. Solentiname is a collection of thirty-eight islands; at that time it held some ninety families composed of farmers, craftspeople, and fisherfolk. Cardenal's homily each Sunday was a dialogue with these persons about ways the gospel affected everyday life. We must remember that in the 1960s Nicaragua remained under the repressive regime of the Somoza family and while Solentiname seemed but a fly speck, it attracted attention as Cardenal published poetry and prose writings from the people in the island villages reflecting on the nature of the Christian gospel. Cardenal noted: "It was the Gospel which radicalized us politically. The peasants began to understand the core of the Gospel message: The announcement of the Kingdom of God, that is, the establishment on this earth of a just society, without exploiters or exploited."[13] Such a radical position was not held in high esteem by President Anastasio Somoza. In October 1977 the regime crushed and burned Solentiname. Those villagers who were not killed joined the Sandinistas, overthrowing Somoza on July 19, 1979. The people returned to Solentiname, and Cardenal became the Sandinista minister of culture, "a post which Cardenal regards as 'priestly' because it deals with total human development through poetry, music, art, film and sports."[14]

One of the paintings done by a Solentiname villager portrays the angel Gabriel's announcement regarding the birth of Jesus to Mary, who is seated at her sewing machine in a simple peasant hut. Reflecting on this passage and this painting, two villagers comment on the nativity. Rebeca says, "From the moment of his birth, God chose conditions like the poorest person's." Felix responds, "The scriptures are perfectly clear. The fact is that Christ was born as a poor little child, like the humblest person. The scriptures keep telling me this, and I don't understand why we don't see it."[15] In commenting on the slaughter of the innocents, a section of the Bible where Herod's troops are engaged in killing children (Matt. 2:12-23), Oscar states:

> Do you know how I understand birth? The birth of a child is very important. . . . I feel this deeply as the father of a family. But that's not the birth that this Gospel is telling us about. Do you know what I understand by the child here? It's the poor people! They are the children with respect to the rich. I mean that we, then, since we're poor, we're children, we're always beneath the rich. It seems to me that's what this birth means, a little child who suffers. We ourselves, even though we're adults, are like children: the poor.[16]

BEING HEARD INTO VOICE

One might debate the pros and cons of the Sandinistas, but of interest here is the process (from having "no voice" to having been "heard into voice," to "speaking" with power) experienced by the peasants of Solentiname. This process could be summarized as follows: First, they shared a *common experience*. Somoza clearly oppressed this village and its people. His violent policies had killed their children and seemingly crippled their existence.

Second, they had a religious *presence* in Ernesto Cardenal, a man who lived a religious tradition. An ancient gospel in the Christian tradition is the *Gospel of Thomas*, which says, "Split the stick and there is Jesus; lift the stone and one finds the Lord" (*Gospel of Thomas* 95:26-28). In part, we can affirm that statement as a correct observation, in that common experience is filled with wonder. But the "split the stick" part is true only for those who are immersed in the interpretive framework of the Christian tradition; that is, the symbolic words used to interpret the experience make sense only to the "insiders" of that particular tradition. If you are a carpenter concerned about the strength of a wooden structure, you share another interpretive framework, and you may "split the stick" and find only termites. The words Jesus and Lord frame the splitting-the-stick experience within a particular faith tradition. Splitting the stick of wood—the experience—reveals its fullness only because I am an insider, immersed in the words I use when I split the stick. The peasants of Solentiname, immersed in this tradition and trustful of their religious leader's presence, split the sticks of their contextual, experiential lives and found Jesus.

They could not have done so unless they had, third, a *hospitable space* within which both experience and the embodiment of a lively religious tradition could be discussed. This is not an easy thing to do. In a brokenhearted world, people are strangers. Strangers are perceived to be just that—potential enemies, sources of brokenheartedness. We don't have to look too far to discover the stranger in our midst. There are strangers in churches, families, even in marriages. "Keeping distance" is a fine art within our brokenhearted world. In contrast, the Bible suggests that it is in welcoming the stranger that we open ourselves to ourselves and to God. Hospitality, the Bible seems to say, is a serious obligation. And who knows, strangers often carry precious gifts with them. Parker Palmer suggests that "to teach is to create a space in which obedience to truth is practiced."[17] For Palmer, hospitality becomes a core concept for creating such a space.

In Solentiname, just such a kind of hospitable opening occurred; Palmer notes the importance of "truth" to such a moment:

> The English word "truth" comes from a Germanic root that also gives rise to our word "troth," as in

the ancient vow "I pledge thee my troth." With this word one person enters into a *covenant* with another, a pledge to engage in a mutually accountable and transforming relationship, a relationship forged of trust and faith in the face of unknowable risks [italics added]."[18]

To engage in *transcendence* (the fourth "core condition" for ministry with young children), is to risk speaking the truth. It is to pledge the openness of my truth (my lived experience, my challenge, my woundedness, and the words I use to give shape to all these things); all this I pledge to share openly in a hospitable way. I "pledge thee—and thee—and thee—my troth."

What happened in Solentiname is clear—the peasants of the islands acted upon what "truth" revealed to them. The "core conditions" of ministry were present. The religious leader was a powerful *presence* who invoked biblical *hospitality* in covenantal conversations around the *contextual experiences* of their lives together. And *transcendence*, the fourth core condition, was expected. The conversations held by these villagers "split the sticks" of their lives, and they were visibly heard into voice through an outpouring of rich, vibrant, politically persuasive paintings. Immersed in the process, they "saw" Jesus.

One of their paintings shows Mary and Joseph fleeing with Jesus into Egypt. Donald, a villager, comments: "You know what country we're in and how there's so much infant mortality, and so many stunted, undernourished children. I think that's persecuting children. I think the same thing is happening here as happened to Christ when he was persecuted as a child."[19] Donald has discovered the "truth" of the gospel as it confronts his reality, and he is transformed.

A second painting envisions Herod massacring all the

infants in Bethlehem, but the troops of Herod (Somoza) are painted as carrying the weapons and wearing the uniforms supplied by the United States of America. Felipe speaks: "And the same thing happens here and in other places, wherever they're screwing the people. The innocent. Because the ones they are killing are the innocent. In all these cases they're killing the child that they don't want to see grown up."[20]

By "speaking such true words," to use Freire's phrase, the world of Solentiname has been "transformed."[21] And the day-to-day activity of the villagers of Solentiname has been forever changed. The sharing of a common experience within a covenantal, hospitable space, the power of a common religious tradition, and a believing leader were able to make this community heard into voice. "Voice," in this instance, is the ongoing activity of creating richly detailed and highly symbolic paintings that confront and communicate their reality, their "truth." And one world was transcended.

THE CONTEMPORARY WORLD

Morton wisely has suggested that being heard into voice is "equivalent to empowerment."[22] She concludes, "we empower the disinherited, the outsider, as we are able to hear them name in their own way their own oppression and suffering."[23] Such "naming," Morton claims, "runs counter to those theologians who claim that God is sometimes silent, hidden, or withdrawn (deus absconditus), and that we must wait patiently until 'He' deigns to speak again."[24] Her argument is provocative. "A more realistic alternative to such despair, or 'dark night of the soul,' would see God as the hearing one—hearing us to our own responsible word."[25] But do we—twentieth-century United States citizens—*believe* that such a being heard into voice is necessary for our modern, technologically oriented lives?

In 1989 a young woman named Laurie Dann made the cover of national newspapers when she entered an elementary school in Winnetka, Illinois, and indiscriminately began to shoot children. Winnetka, an upper-middle-class suburb of Chicago, is a long way from the village of Solentiname, Nicaragua, but Marcia Heeter, minister of spiritual life in the Winnetka Presbyterian Church, reflects upon the role that church chose to play as she recalls the horrible impact of that day:

One Friday morning terror struck my community when a young woman entered a grade school and shot several children. That afternoon people began to call the church asking what we were doing and if we could have some kind of service that night. At four P.M. the head pastor and I called the deacons and had them call everyone in the 450-member congregation and tell them we were having a service that evening at seven. We decided to have a Quaker-type service, inviting people to share what had been going on with them in relation to the shooting.

After people gathered that evening, I shared my experience of standing outside the school much of the afternoon. Bob [the senior pastor] shared his experience, which included a few moments with the principal, a steady visitor to our church. Then we invited others to share, to read scripture of their choice, or to request a song of their choice to be sung together.

We sat in silence and tears much of the time, allowing the sanctuary to be a container for our pain. Bob and I sat in chairs in front of the congregation at their same level to symbolize our connection with the people. After much debate I had gone along with his strong preference that we wear robes symbolizing God's presence among us. So there we were, the "children of God," gathered in pain and sorrow.

About 100 people came, children, teachers from the school, teachers from other schools, families, nonchurch members, and some who had no connection to schools but wanted to be with those who were closer to the event. Many stayed after the service and talked to each other for a long time. In response to the initiative of that initial person who called—a person of faith—the church provided a ritual to hold and to express the shared experience. This ritual began a longer process for the church—individually and collectively—responding to the terror. The process continues in other forms: in sermons, in adult education, and in discussions within small groups.[26]

Unfortunately the religious community often remains silent, refusing to play its powerful role within society; all too often it has "identified with the oppressor" and lost its "voice." Marcia Heeter, however, relates the story of how one congregation in one community—Winnetka, in the grip of the "Lauri Dann" incident—responded with an intentional invocation of "sacred space." Whatever had been the "domesticated" agenda for that day was scrapped in light of this immediate and terrifying experience. Religious leaders asked, "In light of our faith, how can we respond? What ought we to do?" And something *was* done. A "sacred space" was constituted so that people in pain might name their experience and discover their "voice."

CRITICAL REFLECTION: THE SACRED CIRCLE

Often it takes a tragedy—like the shooting in Winnetka or Solentiname under Somoza—to intrude into and overcome our fear of the sacred. In the meantime, we are kept numb by our modern ability to split reality into the "sacred" and the "secular." Perhaps, by dividing the world into two separate realms we exercise our modern presumption that somehow we are in control and that anything pertaining to the sacred is to be rejected as fevered gibberish. The secular world honors hard, scientific data. Things sacred are usually considered to be fuzzy and without adequate proof. Things sacred occur on Sunday; we engage in the secular world Monday through Saturday. Native Americans often are confused by the seemingly arbitrary nature of this position. There is no such sacred–secular split for the Native American. While personal interpretations and cosmologies sometimes differ, Native Americans traditionally have held to a more integrated understanding of the nature of the universe than have Americans of European descent. This holistic sense of life can be sensed in the Navaho "Night Chant":

> *In beauty I walk.*
> *With beauty before me, I walk.*
> *With beauty behind me, I walk.*
> *With beauty below me, I walk.*
> *With beauty above me, I walk.*
> *With beauty all around me, I walk.*
> *It is finished in beauty,*
> *It is finished in beauty.*[27]

"Beauty" in this poem is much more than aesthetic appreciation of nature; it is a condition more easily likened to understanding, knowing, and sensing one's place within the universe. Immersed in such beauty, there is no room for the Native American to engage in the faulty splitting of reality into spheres arbitrarily labeled secular and sacred. Beauty surrounds and interpenetrates the Native American.

Nonetheless, there are certain occasions, certain moments in life, that call for *intentionality* on the part of religious leaders. Winnetka was one such moment. For such moments, a "sacred circle" is drawn. And when the Native American draws the sacred circle on the ground and steps inside, it is with the knowledge that certain chants will be employed today, because it is a particular season or occasion for which the sacred circle has been drawn. This means that not only certain chants, but certain invocations, insights, and specific pieces of equipment will be employed today. One does not bring one color of sand to the circle if another is called for.

Anthropology is helpful here. Anthropologists speak of "liminality."[28] When the sacred circle is drawn and we, both individuals and groups, step inside, all the old structures are understood to be in flux and a kind of "up in the air" transcendent openness ("liminality") occurs as old personal and social interpretations of meaning are challenged. At the same time, the boundaries of the sacred circle guarantee—because of a shared tradition—that no one inside will be destroyed. The mysterious result is that often, as a result of experiencing sacred space, the place where we once located ourselves no longer makes sense; we have experienced transcendence.

Unfortunately American religious leaders, by accepting other metaphors as normative, have been (for the most part) cut off from this powerful process of drawing sacred circles. While Marcia Heeter and Bob Hudnut did indeed name the experience of tragedy for their Winnetka community, few religious leaders speak or act that way. It appears that "truth" is to be found in more practical, worldly-wise endeavors. To return to the discussion provoked by John Dewey in chapter 1, the authors believe that all experience can be understood to be religious. This includes the painful experience of Winnetka. As religious educators, we must be presences who stand with children and their experiences, both good and bad, while creating hospitable space within which transcendence occurs. These are core conditions for ministry with young children. In addition, *educare* means "to lead out." Leading out, hearing others into voice, engaging in the truth-telling, naming process of individuals or a faith community on pilgrimage—these are alternative ways to describe the intentional, ongoing congregational process of religious education. If it is to avoid the sacred/secular split, religious education will connect with the whole living, breathing, meaning-making person, not just the information-processing person. This means that education, if it is "religious," must deal not only with the positive but also with the hurtful experiences of life.

Because such experiences—both negative and positive—involve transcendence, they are religious. The authors believe that the religious educator can be understood to be an adult who believes in the transcendent God and who is intimately involved with establishing the nurturing and challenging boundaries of sacred space. Thus the teacher becomes a ritual elder who not only invokes the sacred circle but also provides powerful texts, symbols, and stories out of the past in preparation for moving across the old, limit-laden boundaries of individuals and the gathered community into the future. This forward movement is into a new situation, not a return to the old. While such sacred space often occurs in worship, we believe that it can also intentionally occur within the Sunday school classroom, the preschool, the parents'-day-out program, the demonstration for fair housing practice, and the happy occasion when the religious teacher or church member meets a child on the street in the neighborhood. We do not believe the use of the term sacred space in this fashion dilutes it; we hold that a reclaiming of the role of ritual elder is essential to an appropriate understanding of what religious educators are called to be and to do.

Education is powerful. To "lead" assumes a vision, and those who educate from within a religious tradition lean—with spirited hope—into the future because of and in response to such vision. God is present here. As religious educators, we can and should invoke sacred space. And, in this process, transformation, surprising and uncontrolled, occurs. The holy is encountered in our shared experience and our very being.

THE GOD WHO LISTENS

This chapter began by indicating that often, when the needs of adults are not met, the adults revert to beastlike behavior and devour their children. Elie Wiesel, a child during World War II, survived the degradation of the Nazi extermination camp at Auschwitz. Years later, he wrote a book in which he recalled returning to his boyhood home.[29] Once home, he dug up in his yard a cherished watch, his Bar Mitzvah watch given to him to remind him that he was responsible to the timeless laws of God. He had buried that watch just before he was herded into the Auschwitz-bound cattle cars. Now digging into the hard, packed soil—a generation later—he found his watch, but it was tarnished, corroded, defiled—just as his memory and spirit had been tarnished, corroded, and defiled by his experience at Auschwitz. With watch in hand, Wiesel cried out to the God who permitted this to happen. He desired an answer from God. Instead, he found a God who has not all the answers but rather a God who has tears in his eyes.

Christians assert that this God with tears in his eyes is the God we meet in Christ on Good Friday of Easter week: a God who does not have all the answers, a God who does not have all power, but a God who meets us with eyes full of tears. This God meets us in every event—even the painful, hurtful ones—of our experience-packed lives. This is the

God, Immanuel, "God with us," who comes as a child in vulnerable solidarity with the creation: "despised and rejected, acquainted with grief," the one who suffers on a cross; the one who cries, "My God, why have you forsaken me?" There is no sufficient answer that can be given in the face of Auschwitz, Winnetka, or the fable of Broccoli Bear. There is, however, the peculiar (seemingly absurd) claim of the Christian church that despite all this pain—nevertheless—the God of covenantal love always stands with us, a God with eyes full of tears who hears us into voice. The educator who claims the adjective "religious" therefore embraces and does not run from the experience of the sacred circle. And there is the claim—a powerful claim— that when we enter the sacred circle and call upon God's name, God responds.

CHAPTER EIGHT

WALKING ON WATER
SHAPING THE CHURCH'S MINISTRY WITH CHILDREN

> *The evolution of humane child care has been glacially slow. In many Third World countries today, the status of children has changed little in the last ten centuries. In abundantly wealthy America, one out of four children goes to bed hungry each night and the death rates of inner-city children now rival those of underdeveloped countries.*
>
> —TIM UNSWORTH, "What the Church Has Taught About Child Care"

In the chaotic center of the storm, Jesus came to the disciples, walking on the water, according to Matthew 14. Storms happen easily in that part of the world. Shallow lakes churn into a boat-tipping frenzy with only a few puffs of wind. No wonder that the ancient Hebrew writers often used water as an indication of chaos. We are not surprised, therefore, when Matthew tells us how the disciples faced a chaotic storm and were surprised to see Jesus, the "Lord of wind and waves, walking on the water," and calling them to do the same. For many children today, life is just such a chaotic storm.[1] Those adults who hear Jesus calling them often are fearful and trembling as they walk out onto these waters into ministry with young children. For example, child-care workers, usually women and often single parents, frequently are paid the minimum wage and receive few, if any, benefits, not even sick leave.[2] For such persons, the storm is very real, and walking on the waters is risky.

At times, however, all of us have stood upon the shore, uncertain whether we have the strength or wherewithal to move onto the "waters"—those tumultuous waves of misunderstanding, red tape, institutionalized egocentrism, inadequate resources, indifference, and at times, overt hostility. We know that the ongoing process of providing humane care for all children is not a high priority in this country, despite all rhetoric to the contrary.[3] Nevertheless, in spite of these difficulties, Jesus continues to call us, asking us to stride out, unafraid, onto the stormy waters. And when we choose to walk onto these waters, we need to remember the biblical story about Jesus "walking on the water," where Peter saw and instantly responded. Boldly stepping onto the water in the middle of the storm, Peter quickly "became afraid" and began to slip beneath the waves.

BEYOND THE LOCAL CHURCH: THE AMERICAN CONTEXT

The Christian tradition claims, however, that when those engaged in ministry "slip beneath the waves," Jesus' outstretched hand will catch them and lift them into the safety of the "boat." The Christian tradition claims through this image that we are not alone in ministry. We can join with others—persons who are in the same, or similar "boats"—and continue our pilgrimage upon the waters. The boat-upon-the-water image has often been used to represent visually the church or local congregations. Yet not every "boat," or local congregation, engages in an intentional ministry with young children. The reality of congregational life is that each congregation, embedded within the social context of this country, has to sort out what it is that might or might not motivate their journey into a ministry with young children, a ministry that currently receives low priority on the cultural agenda.

As congregations sort out their reasons for such a ministry, the authors identify two major *dilemmas* facing them. In using the term dilemma, we draw upon the work of Ann and Harold Berlak.[4] For the Berlaks, dilemmas are contradictions that emerge within a society. Suggesting that societal change occurs when people become aware of conflicting understandings of reality, the Berlaks present a strong case toward naming and critically reflecting upon such dilemmas.

THE DILEMMA OF RECONCILING THE SEPARATION OF CHURCH AND STATE WITH A "WHOLE CHILD" PERSPECTIVE

An initial dilemma facing those who "walk onto the waters" in ministry with young children in the American context is that: while Americans ground educational practice in a sharp separation of church and state, at the same time those who work with young children realize, out of a "whole child" perspective, that it is impossible to avoid "the religious" in the life of a young child (see chapter 1). This means, for example, that while the religious experiences of young children are often clearly visible to those who work with them, early-childhood programs receiving public funding are prohibited by law from using overt religious language. These restrictions deny the adult any involvement with what appears to be a major part of a child's experience in order to carry out the deep commitment in this country toward avoiding the particular claims of religions within public education.

Congregations sponsoring preschool programs sometimes attempt to "solve" this dilemma by housing *both* government-sponsored preschools (where no "religious language" is allowed) and church-sponsored preschools (where religious language is sometimes emphasized). Usually the church-sponsored preschool is understood to be part of the "mission" of the church while the government-sponsored preschool is referred to as a "secular agency renting space" in the church, not a part in any way of the church's mission. This, to the authors' minds, is not a satisfactory solution.

So what can the church, the teacher or care giver, and the

parent do? While the dilemma cannot be solved, we can work within it toward needed change. Chapter 4 presented four core conditions for ministry with young children. These conditions *operate the same way in both government and church-sponsored preschool settings.* The authors argue that critical reflection on these conditions by church, care givers, preschool directors, and parents could provide a way to interpret both the "secular" and "religious" preschools housed in a church. Those conditions include: (1) being informed by the *context* of the child, (2) creating and sustaining *hospitable space*, (3) providing a caring and competent *adult presence*, and (4) encouraging and nurturing the child's ongoing process of *transcendence.* These conditions hold for the hospital, the public school, the parochial school, and the social-service agency, as well as the church-sponsored preschool. Through these four conditions adults can begin to sense what it means to "practice the presence of God" in the lives of young children.[5]

THE DILEMMA OF VALUING A PARTICULAR FAITH PERSPECTIVE IN A PLURALISTIC WORLD

Such "practice," however, is usually informed by specific understandings about who or what "God" is and is therefore embodied in quite different ways. Within the Christian tradition, to minister is actively to incarnate the human face of God (see chapter 5). Such ministry builds upon *transcendence* in the life process and relies upon a *covenantal* understanding of reality (see chapter 1). It is from within these "understandings," or assumptions, that we flesh out the specific shape of our ministry with young children. We therefore could be said to have drawn upon a selective set of resources acceptable, interesting, and challenging to us because of our Christian view of reality. Our "ministry" looks a certain way because of these understandings, assumptions, and resources. In other words, we have assumed that an activist, transcendent, co-creative kind of role will occur for teachers and care givers who engage in ministry with young children from a Christian perspective (Gen. 1:26). Other faiths, however, might not understand or accept either this language or the tradition it represents. A second dilemma might therefore be expressed as follows: "We value and in fact assign meaning to all of life out of our Christian stance; yet we also want all children to thrive and grow within a culturally diverse world." We must be careful here, since this second dilemma occurs in large part because the sense of self evolves differently in different cultures. There are, for example, cultural differences in the ways groups of persons balance the continual tension that always exists between being a member of a group and being an individual. Howard Gardner helps us better understand this tension and its various resolutions as he compares and contrasts "particle" and "field" societies: "In a particle society like our own, the focus of the self inheres primarily in the specific individual. . . . There is an associated interest, even a fascination, with the isolated individual person."[6] In contrast to the particle society, Gardner suggests that in the *field* society the "locus of attention, power and control is placed in the hands of other people or even of the society as a whole."[7]

With the specific history and societal configurations drawn from the Western tradition, the United States is a good example of a particle society (we put a high priority on the individual's autonomy). When, however, a specific history and social configuration is grounded in traditions other than ours, the sense of self may differ. For example, China tends to emphasize social conformity over individual autonomy. It might be understood as a good example of a *field* society. Such differing conceptualizations of the self develop from and are fostered by the dominant faiths within differing cultures. The Judeo-Christian emphasis on the *individual* has affected this country; the Maoist-Confucian emphasis on the *group* has affected China. Again, we commit a grave error when we expect others' experience of reality to mirror our own. Such cultural differences lie at the core of the sense of self. The experiences we assign religious meaning to and come to understand, *given our cultural perception of reality*, may be viewed differently by others.

Ministry with young children in pluralistic settings, therefore, should not be an occasion for conversion. In addition, a true ministry with young children occurs through the four conditions listed above in this chapter and is not determined to be "ministry" by the presence or absence of particular words or symbols. In other words, Christians who work and care for children in pluralistic, avowedly "secular" settings can be engaging in ministry as much as those who serve in avowedly "religious" settings. In both settings, helpful "ministry" occurs through the positive interventions made within the experience of those young children. Ministry is carried more by being on the side of transcendence than by the use of conversion strategies or the presence or absence of particular words or symbols.

The same definition of a positive ministry holds true for those programs for young children *internal* to the life of the faithful community. This means that young children are connected within a particular faith tradition more by the experience of belonging to a "faith" than by being targeted for conversion, information, or particular words. Throughout this book the authors have argued that a congregation true to itself will affect young children through the ways it engages its reality; children will grow within a *particular* tradition's interpretation of reality most powerfully as they experience that interpretation through sharing in the experiential activities of people of faith. Intentional "religious education" with young children, therefore, is not so much a matter of transmitting information through a specific denominational curriculum as the building of a scaffolding that encourages young children to become involved in those "faithing" activities that nurture and challenge them. A faithful congregation will be engaged in many such "faithing" activities.[8]

A Sunday school that understands itself to be the primary and only agency through which a congregation's religious education for young children will occur is, therefore, to our minds, counterproductive to the multifaceted possibilities present within the congregation (see chapter 5). And while worship is not an educational "tool," we believe that adults who worship and share affirming, hope-filled experiences with children are passing from one generation to another a particular faith tradition's language, story, and symbols (see chapter 6). C. Ellis Nelson phrases it like this: "The issue is not whether preaching *or* teaching is the preferred means of communication of the gospel, but how congregations can become aware of the presence of Christ and become more dedicated to being the body of Christ in our secular society."[9]

TOWARD CONGREGATIONALLY CENTERED RELIGIOUS EDUCATION

At best, those captured by the cultural assumptions of the school cannot see the forest for the trees. At worst, they see and understand but labor on, too frightened to consider alternative options. Such fright, however, cannot help the religious educator who is trying to be faithful but who understands that, come fall, the congregation assumes that there will be in place a fully staffed, age-graded, professionally administered Sunday *school*. While there is no set "cure" for this assumption, the authors believe change will occur only when the pastor of the congregation is willing to engage a core group of persons—including those currently charged with the responsibility for religious education—within the process of seeing in a new way the congregation's multifaceted educational mission.

Through conversations and correspondence with three midwestern religious educators, the authors have come to believe that such congregational change occurs in three stages: (1) maintenance, (2) transition, and (3) congregationally centered religious education. Betty, a recent seminary graduate called as the associate pastor in a twelve-hundred member congregation, carries the title of youth minister and director of Christian education.[10] She exclaims,

You were right about the importance of *maintenance*. People are starting to trust me, and that's primarily because their last associate came in and made changes all over the place. He lasted two years and then left. When I got here, I listened. I quickly discovered that the Christian education committee was in disarray. No one knew what to do, other than expecting me to "pick up the pieces" and arrive at September with the Sunday school all set to go. When I asked, "Why Sunday school?" no one had what I'd call a good response. Most of them were variations of "that's what we've always done," but I decided it was too early to tackle this issue head-on, so I scrambled a lot that summer and in fact discovered some neat folk and was able to rebuild both the committee and the Sunday school by September 10! But I was exhausted, and more than a bit angry at some of the mindlessness connected with this whole situation.

Nevertheless, this first year has been a time of maintaining the school as the educational form of the congregation. Along the way, however, I moved beyond the Sunday hour block of time—we had occasional pizza and salad meetings with the teachers, both for morale and for my getting to know them better. I pushed toward a summer intergenerational "family camp" as an initial experiment, and the core group pulled it off rather well. We got the pastor involved and wound up the week with a powerful Sunday intergenerational worship service. I guess I was able to do that because by mid-year I felt I had a handle on what was going on in the congregation, that I had the support of the pastor, and that the Christian education committee was just beginning to understand that there are a variety of approaches to Christian education, not just the school. I came to understand that when C.E. is always and only associated with the school, there has to be a lot of trust in anyone who asks "Why is that?" Otherwise, it's "Goodbye associate pastor." So I took my time, held my breath, stirred up a lot of discussion about alternative possibilities, and actually held what I sense is our first step away from the school, our summer family camp.

Betty is a good example of the initial stage of the intentional "maintenance" process a congregation needs to engage in if it intends eventually to have a more holistic vision of religious education within the congregation. In this stage the religious educator *maintains* that which is present. In fact, Betty had to pull together a new committee and school. This suggests three things: (1) the initial task is not to challenge but to listen to the congregational story; (2) such listening identifies educational forms that need maintenance and gives the Christian educator an opportunity to demonstrate competence and caring; (3) within the act of maintenance, the interplay among the educator, the pastor, and the appropriate core groupings of laity creates a work-ing relationship sufficient to initiate some new "experiments," like Betty's "family camp." What is done in this stage is not as important as listening, gaining a working relationship, and demonstrating competence and caring. While the "Maintenance Stage" isn't a time for major innovations, it can be perceived by the religious educator as a time to lay the groundwork for an ensuing change.

The dangers associated with this first stage focus upon the seductiveness of the idea of school. Once the deadlines, the curriculum, and the people are in place, the religious educator reaches a kind of "comfort zone" within which everything "fits." When this occurs, the school can begin to function as a well-oiled machine, and the director can settle back and administer.

David, however, the sole pastor in a two-hundred-member town congregation, wrote Bill the following letter in which he clearly spelled out how he avoided becoming trapped in the maintenance stage. David seems to be in a second stage, that of the *transitional*:

> When I got here five years ago, the Sunday school was the totality of the Christian education effort. The good thing about this was that everyone came together for both the school and the worship that followed. The negative things included the fact that the Sunday school used a very rigid Sunday school curriculum, was still tightly age-graded, and rarely experienced worship as being connected with what happened in church school. I have to admit, however, that in my first three years, this congregation taught me an incredible amount about the importance of the Sunday school in their life. This surprised me because I was raised in one of those big congregations where I rarely knew anyone outside the experience of the immediate classroom. So, once

I felt I had congregational support, I started to hold regular one-day "retreats" in which we discussed a wide range of "identity" topics. And one day, when I asked members of the church to tell me what they hoped to see happen in Sunday school, one older guy said that he felt Sunday school was one of the ways God "broke bread" *within* the congregation. So when I asked why—if that was the case—there never was a link up between the Sunday school curriculum material and the Sunday sermon, this same guy said, "Because the pastor preceding our last pastor never knew until Sunday morning what his sermon topic might be." Aha! It was then that I understood the importance of congregational story; but, more to the point of my letter, it was at that moment when I recognized that this congregation expected more of me—that they were ready to try some new possibilities. Well, we played with ways we might intentionally work at being the bread both within and outside the congregation. And someone said that he felt the natural link that was missing was the sermon *acting in concert with* the church school discussion.

David's congregation experimented with (1) a lectionary-based curriculum linking Sunday's sermon to the Sunday school, (2) four intergenerational church-sponsored events (a fall rally, an Advent workshop, a Lenten exploration, and an Easter celebration) in which worship and Sunday school came together, and (3) a worship "feedback-feedforward" once a month in which participants discussed current topics (not lectionary-bound) in Sunday school and then met for lunch and conversation following the sermon, which would also center upon the chosen topic.

David's case clearly moves beyond Betty. While Betty is involved with the process of *maintenance*, David has moved, with the wholehearted approval and commitment of his congregation, into the second stage—the *transitional*. Here major steps are being taken, yet no one can begin to predict their exact outcome. It is obvious, however, that this is a dangerous time for David and the congregation. Transformative change is always unsettling, particularly when a congregation is moving in what looks like several directions at the same time. There will be persons from this congregation who will be heard to say, "I liked it better the old way."

The third stage, the congregationally centered education model, also tries out "new things," but it isn't so "up in the air." The congregation has grown together into a cohesive understanding of religious education, which now informs their ministry. For example, Sarah, pastor of a 342-member congregation, notes that she has been there for six years:

> I can now say that I was regarded by the congregation as an experiment. I was a woman, and they weren't certain what I might do as a pastor, but both sides have been pleasantly surprised. I supported their Sunday school, though it was small, as well as the one adult study group, even though it was ingrown. In my third year the study group asked me to present a theological study on baptism, communion, and discipleship. This went on for six weeks, and in the middle of the study one of the sons of a church leader was killed in a farming accident. While this was at once a painful experience, it also mobilized our study group into an intentional expression of the issues we were studying.
>
> Facing this tragedy quickly got beyond the printed page, if you know what I mean. Following that occasion, eight adults formed a morning prayer

group that met with me once a week. Sometimes groups like this are either ineffectual or problematic within the congregation, but this group became salt and leaven inside and outside our congregation. They identified children and family concerns as the issue facing both our congregation and our larger community. And we've moved along a route of considering every move in light of our faith's tradition. Now I can look back at those times as the moment we began to think about the congregational implications of religious education. Out of that slim start we've (1) gotten children into worship in very natural and affirming ways, (2) started, as a mission of the church, a preschool center, as well as a mothers' morning-out program, and (3) linked our support to the family health center recently established—with our help—within our county. We are now working on youth programming and job training within our essentially rural area. Do you catch my enthusiasm? And we've done all this in ways that have spilled over into every area of our congregation. After saying all this, I think the best thing that has happened to me was a gift from a young girl who stepped close one Sunday and said, very shyly, "I liked the song we sang in church today." Six years ago someone that age would not have been in worship. Today, her presence is a given.

In this third stage, despite the idiosyncratic ways congregations get there, they have discovered what C. Ellis Nelson has called "the Corinthian principles": (1) Paul considered the church at Corinth to be "a place where individuals learned to practice their faith," (2) Paul assumed that the Corinthian church's worldview would be at odds with "the culturally formed mind-set of the Greeks and interpreted the gospel within those assumptions," (3) "within a congregational context, Paul unified experience with tradition," and (4) Paul expected the congregation at Corinth "to generate practical theology about its life situation."[11] When connected to children, these principles suggest that children are educated in the faith most appropriately when they are relationally connected with adults in activities prized by those adults. A congregation so involved cannot contain all of the educational forms it might value within the Sunday school; while the authors cannot offer a step-by-step procedure, by reflecting on churches both historic (Corinth) and contemporary (Betty, David, and Sarah's congregations), we can begin to recognize how a congregation's life and practice (connecting with caring adults, hospital, preschool, Sunday school, worship, and congregational style) educates our children.

A LITANY FOR THE WORLD'S CHILDREN

As the authors conclude this book, we are reminded that "Bulletproof back-to-school clothes are the latest thing for New York City children who run a dangerous gauntlet to and from class."[12] Perhaps this is a glimpse of our future. But we are also reminded that at a conference on "The World's Religions for the World's Children," representatives of twelve religions in forty countries adopted the following supplication for the world's children. We believe it catches what we hope is the spirit of this book. It begins with these four lines: "The child has the breath and spirit of life. The child, present here and now, is the past embodied and the future becoming. The child wants to survive, to be protected, to develop. The child needs peace, with justice and freedom." These lines emphasize that ministry with children is the common cause of all peoples. But the lines that follow suggest that those who "minister" with young children are not alone. In the language of this book, God walks with them on the water. Hear these lines in a spirit of prayer:

Save Our Children
Tortured by hunger and thirst
  Save our Children
Ravaged from preventable disease
  Save our Children
Mutilated by cruel customs and practices
  Save our Children
Savaged by the brutalities of war
  Save our Children
Victimized by violence
  Save our Children
Broken by exploitative child labor
  Save our Children
Traumatized by sexual abuse
  Save our Children
Damaged by drug abuse
  Save our Children
Poisoned by environmental pollution
  Save our Children

Protect Our Children
Stunted with suffering
  Protect our Children
Rejected without name
  Protect our Children
Denied belonging
  Protect our Children
Withered without hope
  Protect our Children
Thwarted by limitation due to race, religion,
age, sex, class or caste

Protect our Children
Refused honor and integrity
Protect our Children
Deprived beauty, joy, laughter
Protect our Children
Uprooted because of war, famine, or disease
Protect our Children
Burdened by debts of preceding generations
Protect our Children
Aged before they could be young
Protect our Children
Denied freedom, justice, and peace
Protect our Children

Care for Our Children
Nurtured by love, upheld by guidance,
*   uplifted by understanding*
Care for our Children
Provided with food, clean water, shelter,
*   clothing, and health needs*
Care for our Children
Enriched by a safe and clean environment
Care for our Children
Empowered by education, challenged by
*   opportunity, and strengthened by*
*   the fullness of rights*
Care for our Children
Encouraged to participate in the polities and
*   economies that shape our future*
Care for our Children
Ensured health and health care
Care for our Children
Enhanced by taking their place in a global family
*   enriched by differences*
Care for our Children

Developed with freedom, justice, and peace
Care for our Children

    The child is life and miracle, beauty and mystery,
fulfillment and promise. Save the child. Protect the child.
Care for the child.[13]

To which we add, "Amen."

NOTES

Chapter I

1. Georgia O'Keeffe, quoted in folder, *Georgia O'Keeffe: The Art Institute of Chicago, March 5–June 19, 1988* (Chicago: Art Institute, 1988).
2. Edward Robinson, *The Original Vision* (New York: Seabury Press, 1983), 32–33.
3. Ibid., 12–13.
4. Douglas Sloan, "Educating for a Public Vision," *The Chicago Theological Seminary Register* 74, no. 1 (Winter 1989): 7.
5. Ibid.
6. Ibid.
7. Martin Lang, *Acquiring Our Image of God: Emotional Basis for Religious Education* (Ramsey, N.J.: Paulist Press, 1983), 41.
8. Erik Erikson, *Insight and Responsibility* (New York: W. W. Norton, 1964), 117.
9. Lang, *Acquiring Our Image of God*, 42.
10. Eugenia Hepworth Berger, *Parents as Partners in Education: The School and Home Working Together*, 2nd ed. (Toronto: Merrill Publishing, 1991), 85.
11. Walter Brueggemann, "The Family as World-Maker," *Journal for Preachers* 7 (Easter 1985): 8–15.
12. Elizabeth Stone, "Stories Make a Family," *The New York Times Magazine*, 24 January 1988, 31.
13. Erikson, *Insight and Responsibility*, 114, 152ff.

14. Robinson, *Original Vision*, 96.
15. James Fowler, *Stages of Faith* (San Francisco: Harper & Row, 1981), 9.
16. Ibid., 9–10.
17. John Dewey, *A Common Faith* (New Haven: Yale University Press, 1934), 1–28.
18. Ibid., 10.
19. Maria Harris, *Teaching and Religious Imagination* (New York: Harper & Row, 1987); and Craig Dykstra, *Vision and Character* (New York: Paulist Press, 1981).
20. Elliot W. Eisner, "Introduction," in *Experience in Art*, Nancy R. Smith (New York: Teachers College Press, 1983), x.
21. Fowler, *Stages of Faith*, 4.
22. Phoebe M. Anderson, *3's in the Christian Community* (Philadelphia: United Church Press, 1960; rev. ed. 1992).
23. Brueggemann, "Family as World-Maker," 8.
24. Ibid.
25. Frank E. Reynolds, "Religious Imagination and the Cultivation of Christian Worlds or, The Minister as Christian Bricoleur," in *The Education of the Practical Theologian*, ed. Don S. Browning, David Polk, and Ian S. Evison (Atlanta, Ga.: Scholars Press, 1989), 93–113.
26. Brueggemann, "Family as World-Maker," 8.
27. Ibid., 9.
28. Ibid., 10.
29. Patricia Polacco, *The Keeping Quilt* (New York: Simon & Schuster, 1988), 4.
30. Ibid., 5.
31. Ibid., 13.
32. Ibid., 20.
33. Ibid., 23–24.
34. Ibid., 27.
35. Ibid., 29.
36. Ibid., 5.

Chapter 2

1. Barbara Kimes Myers and Shirley Morgenthaler, "The Development of a Sense of Faith: A Curriculum Concern for Early Childhood Professionals" (unpublished manuscript available from Barbara Kimes Myers, DePaul University, Chicago).

2. Bernard J. F. Lonergan, S.J., *Method in Theology* (New York: Herder & Herder, 1972), 104.

3. Ibid., 111.

4. Philip H. Phenix, "Transcendence and the Curriculum," in *Conflicting Conceptions of Curriculum*, ed. Elliott W. Eisner and Elizabeth Vallance (Berkeley: McCutchan Publishing, 1974), 122.

5. Ibid., 118.

6. Ibid.

7. Ibid., 119.

8. Ibid.

9. Ibid.

10. Jerome Berryman, "Children's Spirituality and Religious Language," *British Journal of Religious Education*, Summer 1985, 126.

11. Robert Coles, interview by Robert Ellsberg, "The Faith of Children," in *Sojourners Magazine*, May 1982, 15.

12. Ibid.

13. Ibid.

14. Ibid., 15–16.

15. Ibid., 16.

16. Ibid.

17. Erik Erikson, *Insight and Responsibility* (New York: W. W. Norton, 1964), 152–153.

18. Erik Erikson, *Childhood and Society*, rev. ed. (New York: W. W. Norton & Co., 1963), 247.

19. Ibid., 118.

20. Margaret Mahler, *On Human Symbiosis and the Vicissitudes of Individuation*, vol. 1 (New York: International Universities Press, 1968).

21. Louise Kaplan, *Oneness and Separateness: From Infant to Individual* (New York: Simon & Schuster, 1978), 186–230.

22. Margaret Wise Brown, *Goodnight Moon*, illus. Clement Hurd (New York: Harper & Brothers, 1947).

23. Ibid., 8.

24. Ibid., 9–12.

25. Ibid., 27–30.

26. Margaret Wise Brown, *The Runaway Bunny*, illus. Clement Hurd (New York: Harper & Brothers, 1942).

27. Ibid., 14–15.

28. Ibid., 30–33.

Chapter 3

1. Will Watterson, "Calvin and Hobbes," a cartoon strip, *Tampa Tribune*, 21 March 1989, sec. E, 1.

2. Will Watterson, "Calvin and Hobbes," a cartoon strip, *Chicago Tribune*, 30 January 1989, sec. 5 ("Tempo"), 7.

3. Philip Greven, *The Protestant Temperament: Patterns of Child-Rearing, Religious Experience, and the Self in Early America* (Chicago: University of Chicago Press, 1977), 62–63.

4. Ibid.

5. Horace Bushnell, *Discourses on Christian Nurture* (New Haven: Yale University Press, 1916), xxxii, and on "original sin," see 15.

6. Ibid., 4, 19.

7. Ibid., 20.

8. Conrad Cherry, ed., *Horace Bushnell: Sermons* (New York: Paulist Press, 1985), 4.

9. Rita Nakashima Brock, *Journeys by Heart: A Christology of Erotic Power* (New York: Crossroad, 1988).

10. "U.S. Lags Behind Counterparts in Care of Children, Report Says," *Chicago Tribune*, 19 March 1990, sec. 1, 5.

11. Brock, *Journeys by Heart*, 3.

12. Ibid., 7.

13. Ibid.

14. Ibid., 8.

15. Ibid., 17.

16. Ibid., 22.

17. Ibid., 45.

18. Eileen W. Lindner, Mary C. Mattis, and June R. Rogers, *When Churches Mind the Children: A Study of Day Care in Local Parishes* (Ypsilanti, Mich.: High Scope Press, 1983), 12.

19. Ibid., 33.

20. Pieces of this chapter, including "Benton," initially appeared as Barbara Kimes Myers and William R. Myers, "Transcendence in the Pre-School: Supporting the Relationship between the Pre-School and the Church," in *British Journal of Religious Education*, Summer 1987, 148–51.

21. Martha Snyder, Ross Snyder, and Ross Snyder, Jr., *The Young Child as Person: Toward the Development of Healthy Conscience* (New York: Human Sciences Press, 233 Spring Street, New York, 10013–1578, 1980), 218. Used by permission.

22. Ibid., 208–9.

23. Ibid., 218.

24. Philip H. Phenix, "Transcendence and the Curriculum," in *Conflicting Conceptions of Curriculum*, ed. Elliott W. Eisner and Elizabeth Vallance (Berkeley: McCutchan Publishing, 1974), 125.

25. Ibid., 131.

26. Ibid., 128.

27. Ibid.

28. Maurice Sendak, *Where the Wild Things Are* (New York: Harper & Row, 1963),1–3.

29. Ibid., 5.

30. Maurice Sendak, interview by Martha Shirk, "Relatively Monstrous," *Chicago Tribune*, 29 January 1990, sec. 3, 2.

31. Sendak, *Where the Wild Things Are*, 20.

32. Ibid., 29.

33. Ibid., 35–37.

34. Ibid., 29, 37.

Chapter 4

1. Ezra Jack Keats, *The Snowy Day* (New York: Viking Press, 1962), back jacket cover.

2. David Bigelow, *Repaired Rainbow*. Bigelow is a midwestern artist whose prints, lithographs, and original works of art are exhibited in numerous galleries and art fairs. His work displays a whimsical approach to life.

3. Andrew D. Lester, *Pastoral Care with Children in Crisis* (Philadelphia: Westminster Press, 1985).

4. Ibid., 135.

5. Audrey Witzman. Used by permission.

6. L. S. Vygotsky, *Mind in Society: The Development of Higher Psychological Processes*, trans. Michael Cole, Vera John-Steiner, Sylvia Scribner, and Ellen Souberman (Cambridge, Mass.: Harvard University Press, 1978).

7. Francine Smolucha, "The Relevance of Vygotsky's Theory of Creative Imagination for Contemporary Research on Play," paper presented at the National Conference of the Society for Research in Child Development (SRCD), Kansas City, Mo., 30 April 1989, 2.

8. Henri J. M. Nouwen, *Reaching Out: The Three Movements*

of the Spiritual Life (Garden City, N.Y.: Doubleday, 1975), 46.

9. Fran Tellner. Used by permission.

10. Ibid.

11. Lester, *Pastoral Care with Children in Crisis*, 135.

12. Lisbeth Schorr and Daniel Schorr, *Within Our Reach: Breaking the Cycle of Disadvantage* (New York: Anchor Press, 1988).

13. Paul Tillich, *Theology of Culture* (New York: Oxford University Press, 1959), 207.

Chapter 5

1. See, for example, William Bigelow, "Inside the Classroom: Social Vision and Critical Pedagogy," *Teachers College Record* 91, no. 3 (Spring 1990): 437–48.

2. C. Ellis Nelson, *How Faith Matures* (Louisville: John Knox Press, 1989), 188.

3. Ibid.

4. Ibid., 196.

5. Charles R. Foster, *Teaching in the Community of Faith* (Nashville: Abingdon Press, 1982), 12.

6. Robert N. Bellah, Richard Madsen, William M. Sullivan, Ann Swidler, and Steven M. Tipson, *Habits of the Heart: Individualism and Commitment in American Life* (Los Angeles: University of California Press, 1985), 142ff.

7. Allen J. Moore, "A Social Theory of Religious Education," in *Religious Education as Social Transformation*, ed. Allen J. Moore (Birmingham: Religious Education Press, 1989), 23.

8. Craig Dykstra, "The Formative Power of the Congregation," in *Religious Education* 82, no. 4 (Fall 1987): 544.

9. V. Bailey Gillespie, *The Experience of Faith* (Birmingham: Religious Education Press, 1988), 34.

10. Ibid., 35.

11. Ibid., 38.

12. Ibid.

13. Nelson, *How Faith Matures*, 89.

14. Dykstra, "Formative Power of the Congregation," 544.

15. Nelson, *How Faith Matures*, 197.

16. Dwayne Huebner, "Religious Education: Practicing the Presence of God," *Religious Education* 82, no. 4 (Fall 1987): 571.

17. Erik H. Erikson and Joan M. Erikson, "On Generativity

and Identity: From a Conversation with Erik and Joan Erikson," *Harvard Educational Review* 51, no. 2 (1981): 249–69.

18. Ibid., 255.

19. Ross Snyder, *Inscape* (Nashville: Abingdon Press, 1968), 37, 40.

20. Huebner, "Religious Education," 573.

21. Ibid., 574.

22. Ibid., 569.

23. Ibid., 570.

24. From a conversation in the D.Min. Intensive class at Chicago Theological Seminary, Fall 1988.

25. Denham Grierson, *Transforming a People of God* (Melbourne: Joint Board of Christian Education of Australia and New Zealand, 1984), 35–36.

26. Gillespie, *Experience of Faith*, 90.

27. Dykstra, "Formative Power of the Congregation," 545.

28. Robert W. Lynn, *Protestant Strategies in Education* (New York: Association Press, 1964), quoted by Dorothy C. Bass, "Teaching with Authority?" *Religious Education* 85, no. 2 (Spring 1990): 305.

29. John H. Westerhoff III, *Will Our Children Have Faith?* (New York: Seabury Press, 1976), 2.

30. Ibid., 66.

31. Ibid., 63.

32. Ibid., 126.

33. Nelson, *How Faith Matures*.

34. Ibid., 151ff.

35. Ibid., 151.

36. Ibid.

37. Ibid., 151ff.

38. Ibid., 230.

39. Based on an experience co-led by Karen Maurer, Homewood Presbyterian Church, Homewood, Ill., and Ruth Craig, Flossmoor Community Church, Flossmoor, Ill.

40. Nelson, *How Faith Matures*, 151.

Chapter 6

1. David Owens, *So That Nothing Is Lost*, sermon at Flossmoor Community Church, Flossmoor, Ill., 4 September 1983, 2. Used by permission.

2. Ibid., 3.

3. Ibid.

4. Phillip Ariès, *Centuries of Childhood: A Social History of Family Life* (New York: Random House, 1962).

5. Joseph F. Kett, *Rites of Passage: Adolescence in America, 1790 to the Present* (New York: Basic Books, 1977).

6. Herbert G. Gutman, *The Black Family in Slavery and Freedom, 1750–1925* (New York: Pantheon Books, 1976).

7. Philip Greven, *The Protestant Temperament: Patterns of Child-Rearing, Religious Experience, and the Self in Early America* (Chicago: University of Chicago Press, 1977).

8. Charles Leslie Glenn, Jr., *The Myth of the Common School* (Amherst: University of Massachusetts Press, 1988).

9. Robert N. Bellah, Richard Madsen, William M. Sullivan, Ann Swidler, and Steven M. Tipton, *Habits of the Heart: Individualism and Commitment in American Life* (Los Angeles: University of California Press, 1985), 298ff.

10. John H. Westerhoff III, *Bringing Up Children in the Christian Faith* (Minneapolis: Winston Press, 1980), 15.

11. Ibid., 16.

12. Ibid.

13. Yvonne White Morey, "Sacred Play: Seeking a Theology of Child," (M.Div. theological position paper, Chicago Theological Seminary, 30 March 1987), 14. Used by permission.

14. Ibid., 15.

15. Donald Ratcliff, "The Cognitive Development of Preschoolers," in *Handbook of Preschool Religious Education*, ed. Donald Ratcliff (Birmingham: Religious Education Press, Inc., 1988), 26. Used by permission.

16. Ibid., 26–27.

17. Ibid., 26.

18. Ibid.

19. Ibid.

20. Ibid.

21. Ibid.

22. Ibid., 27.

23. Ibid.

24. Ibid.

25. Elizabeth McMahon Jeep, "A Look at Questions for the Future: The Eucharist," in *The Sacred Play of Children*, ed. Diane Apostolos-Cappadona (New York: Seabury Press, 1983), 40.

26. *Griggs Educational Service*, Donald Griggs and Patricia

Griggs, 638 Escondido Circle, Livermore, CA 94550, (415) 443–4147.

27. Shepherd of the Hills Presbyterian Church (organizing pastor, Dr. Gregory Clark; the church is in the Presbytery of San Francisco).

28. Donald Griggs and Patricia Griggs, "Adults Intend for Worship to Be Hospitable for Children," copyright 1991. Written for this book. Used by permission.

29. The Presbyterian Church (USA), *Directory for Worship* (W-3. 1004).

30. Griggs and Griggs, "Worship to Be Hospitable for Children."

31. Parts of this section were initially printed as an essay by William R. Myers, "Longer Ropes and Stronger Stakes . . . ," in *Tents, Stores and Stories: Effective Christian Education in the Parish* (New York: United Church Board for Homeland Ministries, 1989), 3–13.

32. Dennis Benson and Stan Stewart, *Star Children* (Nashville: Abingdon Press, 1978). Used by permission.

33. Ibid.

Chapter 7

1. Berke Breathed, "Bloom County," a cartoon strip, *Chicago Sun-Times*, 8 December 1988, 82.

2. Ibid.

3. Quoted by Mary Rose O'Reilley in "The Centered Classroom: Meditations on Teaching and Learning," in *Weavings* 4, no. 5 (September/October 1989): 21–22.

4. Robert Blau and William Recktenwald, "Child-Abuse Deaths up 70% in City," *Chicago Tribune*, 20 May 1990, 1.

5. Ibid.

6. Ibid.

7. Kenneth Eskey, "Let's Focus on Kids, Not the Elderly," *Cleveland Plain Dealer*, 29 October 1989, sec. E, 1.

8. "International Children's Crusade," *Newsweek*, 8 October 1990, 48, a report on the World Summit for Children using statistics from UNICEF, the World Health Organization, and UNESCO. Used by permission.

9. Paulo Freire, *Pedagogy of the Oppressed* (New York: Seabury Press, 1973), 75.

10. Ibid., 97.

11. Nelle Morton, *The Journey Is Home* (Boston: Beacon Press, 1985), 127.

12. Philip Scharper and Sally Scharper, eds., *The Gospel in Art by the Peasants of Solentiname* (Maryknoll, N.Y.: Orbis Books, 1984).

13. Ibid., back cover.

14. Ibid.

15. Ibid., 10.

16. Ibid., 18.

17. Parker Palmer, *To Know as We Are Known: A Spirituality of Education* (San Francisco: Harper & Row, 1983), 69.

18. Ibid., 31.

19. Scharper and Scharper, *Gospel in Art*, 16.

20. Ibid., 18.

21. Freire, *Pedagogy of the Oppressed*, 75.

22. Morton, *The Journey Is Home*, 128.

23. Ibid.

24. Ibid., 129.

25. Ibid.

26. Marcia Heeter (paper, Chicago Theological Seminary, 1989–90). Used by permission. The Lauri Dann incident is documented in Joel Kaplan, George Papajohn, and Eric Zorn, *Murder of Innocence* (Warner Brothers, 1990).

27. Washington Matthews, *The Night Chant, a Navaho Ceremony*, vol. 6 of *Memoirs of the American Museum of Natural History* (New York: Knickerbocker Press, 1902), 145.

28. See, for example, Robert L. Moore, "Space and Transformation in Human Experience," in *Anthropology and the Study of Religion*, ed. Robert L. Moore and Frank E. Reynolds (Chicago: Center for the Scientific Study of Religion, 1984), 126–43.

29. Elie Wiesel, *One Generation After* (New York: Avon Books, 1972), 79–86.

Chapter 8

1. See Tim Unsworth, "What the Church Has Taught About Child Care," *SALT* 9 (November–December 1989): 13; or Children's Defense Fund, *A Call for Action to Make Our Nation Safe for Children: A Briefing Book on the Status of American Children in 1988* (Washington, D.C.: Children's Defense Fund, 122 C. Street, N.W., 20001, 1988), iii.

2. Children's Defense Fund, *A Call for Action*, iii.

3. As of this writing, the first comprehensive child care bill in fty years has passed Congress. There is much to be done 'watchdogging" this legislation.

4. Ann Berlak and Howard Berlak, *Dilemmas of Schooling* (London: Methuen Press, 1981).

5. Dwayne Huebner, "Religious Education: Practicing the Presence of God," *Religious Education* 82, no. 4:569–77.

6. Howard Gardner, *To Open Minds: Chinese Cues to the Dilemma of Contemporary Education* (New York: Basic Books, 1989).

7. Howard Gardner, *Frames of Mind: The Theory of Multiple Intelligences* (New York: Basic Books, 1983).

8. We use "faithing" in the same spirit of James W. Fowler, who suggests that faith is a *verb* in *Stages of Faith: The Psychology of Human Development and the Quest for Meaning* (New York: Harper & Row, 1981), 16.

9. C. Ellis Nelson, *How Faith Matures* (Louisville: John Knox Press, 1989), 228.

10. Betty, David, and Sarah are composites drawn from discussions with Doctor of Ministry students at Chicago Theological Seminary, 1986–1990.

11. Nelson, *How Faith Matures*, 213–17.

12. "Protection for the Mean Streets: Bulletproof School Wear Gives N.Y. Parents Peace of Mind," *Chicago Tribune*, 9 September 1990, sec. 1, 16.

13. Taken from "The World's Religions for the World's Children" Conference, Princeton, N.J., July 25–27, 1990, as reported in *Monday Morning: A Magazine for Presbyterian Leaders* 55, no. 14 (10 September 1990):